The Wrong Bottom Line

The Wrong Bottom Line

and How to Change It

Roy L. Rummler, BS, MME, Ed.D.

iUniverse, Inc.
New York Lincoln Shanghai

The Wrong Bottom Line
and How to Change It

iUniverse books may be ordered through booksellers or by contacting:

iUniverse
2021 Pine Lake Road, Suite 100
Lincoln, NE 68512
www.iuniverse.com
1-800-Authors (1-800-288-4677)

ISBN-13: 978-0-595-41567-0 (pbk)
ISBN-13: 978-0-595-85913-9 (ebk)
ISBN-10: 0-595-41567-9 (pbk)
ISBN-10: 0-595-85913-5 (ebk)

Printed in the United States of America

CONTENT

FOREWORD   FOSTER W. CLINE, M.D. xi

CHAPTER 1   OVERVIEW 1
Why This Book 1
Who This Book is For 3
What You Can Expect 4
The Need To Focus 5
Application and Change 5
An Adventure: Perspectives 6

CHAPTER 2   PREPARATION 8
Do It 9
Be It 9
Summary 9

CHAPTER 3   LEARNING 11
A Key Principle of Leadership and Progress 11
Learner-Teacher-Learner 11
Pay Attention 13
Change Activity 1 14
Change Activity 2 14
Application 15
Stand Back and Look—A Fly on the Wall 16
Change Activity 3 16
Change Activity 4 17
Application 18
Listen 18
Change Activity 5 and Application 20

CHAPTER 4   LOGICAL THINKING 22

Think Ahead 23

Change Activity 6 24

Application 24

Perspective 25

Summary 27

Change Activity 7 29

Change Activity 8 29

Change Activity 9 30

CHAPTER 5   UNDERSTANDING YOUR ROLE 32

Setting a New Profile 32

There Are Always Leaders 32

The Misunderstood Role 33

If They Are Not Following, You Are Not Leading 33

Improving Leadership 35

Change Activity 10 35

Application 37

Change Activity 11 37

Follow Up 39

Leadership Changes Lives 40

Qualities of Leadership 40

Change Activity 12 42

Application 43

Humility 44

Integrity 45

Vision and a Plan 47

A Coach 47

Wise Choices—The Exponential Quality 48

Courage 49

Change Activity 13 50

Change Activity 14 51

Using the Information 53

The Power of Your Position 53

Summary 54

Change Activity 15 55

Application 55

CHAPTER 6   DEALING WITH PERCEPTION 56

The Significance of Perception—As a Man Thinketh 56

Perception is Fact 56

Change Activity 16 58

Thinking and Learning Styles 59

Change Activity 17 60

Change Activity 18 61

Power of The Three Perceptions 63

Change Activity 19 63

Application 65

Perceptions Can Be Changed 65

Assumption: Spongy Ground 66

Change Activity 20 67

Change Activity 21 68

Change Activity 22 69

Application 69

The Power of Perception—Thinking Outside the Box 69

Application 70

CHAPTER 7   THE MOST EXPANDABLE ASSETS 71

People 72

Change Activity 23 73

Change Activity 24 74

Change Activity 25—Reflection 74

Get To Know Your People 75

How We Know Who We Are 76

Names 76

Change Activity 26 76

Application 77

Attention 77

Time 78

Change Activity 27 79

Higher = More Impact 80

Change Activity 28 81

Application 82

Organization or Insulation 83

Validation—View it From Their Shoes 84

Change Activity 29 86

Change Activity 30 88

No One is Perfect 88

Change Activity 31 89

CHAPTER 8   MAXIMIZING THAT ASSET 90

Change Activity 32 90

Introduction 91

Good Coaches Excite and Empower 92

Change Activity 33 93

Do Unto Others 94

Trust, the Sacred Concept 95

Building on Strengths 97

Change Activity 34 98

Assume They Can: Expectations=Performance 99

Application 100

CHAPTER 9   EFFECTIVE COMMUNICATIONS 101

Change Activity 35 103

Application 104

We Communicate All of the Time 104

Basic Elements 105

Change Activity 36 107

Application 108

Let Someone Else Read it 109

Change Activity 37 109

Application 110

Consider (to yourself) Before You Leap 110

No One Knows What You Think, Only What You Say 110

Combining Direct and Indirect 111

Change Activity 38 112

Communication and Accountability 114

Change Activity 39 114

Summary 116

CHAPTER 10   MAKING CHANGES 117

The Difference That Makes the Difference 117

Reasons Changes Do Not Happen 118

The Most Difficult Object to Change 121

Change Is Difficult 121

Change Activity 40 122

Application 123

CHAPTER 11   PLANNING, GOALS AND MEETINGS 125

A Process Not a Program 125

Change Activity 41 126

Change Activity 42 128

Application 128

Change Activity 43 129

Change Activity 44 130

Application 130

Rules of the Road 130

Summary 136

Change Activity 45 137

CHAPTER 12   DIFFERENCES AND DISPUTES 139

The Good, Bad and Ugly 139

Change Activity 46 140

Styles 143

Change Activity 47 145

Application 146

Principles For Smoother Operation 147

Decisions That Stick 148

Dealing with Issues 149

Distributive Bargaining 149

Change Activity 48 150

Change Activity 49 151

Cooperative Bargaining 151

Summary 157

Application 158

CHAPTER 13   BECOMING 161

Serving 163

Inviting 164

The Bridge 167

Everything Was Always Possible 168

Just Do it 169

Being 170

NOTES 173

INDEX 177

FOREWORD

This is a small book packed with large ideas; a short book long on powerful leadership opportunities.

Roy Rummler's years of experience shine through with practical information about effective organizational leadership. *The Wrong Bottom Line* underscores the truth that every organization's most important product is the satisfaction, allegiance, and growth of its employees and staff. Certainly most are aware of the effect of leadership on employee behavior. But *how* exactly do leaders fuel the fire of effective production? How do they encourage staff to come up with great and innovative ideas? How do they encourage, guide, and provide the milieu within which staff and employees thrive?

The Wrong Bottom Line, and How To Change It is a handbook of leadership effectiveness.

The book is devoted to dissecting and solving real problems..

Metaphors and examples are essential to illustrate basic concepts. This book is full of them. On perusing this book you will find understandings that lurked in the back of your mind suddenly illuminated in the full light of conscious recognition. For instance, Dr. Rummler reminds us that the leadership position *itself* has a hidden benefit. When a leader helps subordinates with their day to day lives, the power exponentially increases. He also helps us communicate *effectively*, not just communicate.

The Wrong Bottom Line is chocked full of essential but often forgotten truths: the dangers of assumptions; the power of perceptions and how do deal with them; the recognition that all great teachers are first great learners and how to effectively learn from others; how to grow trust and productivity by building on strengths; recognizing the basic desire of almost everyone to make their lives in the workplace more meaningful.

Any book on leadership has to be filled with the nuts and bolts of effective responses. Here The *Wrong Bottom Line* shines. Dr. Rummler understands that change is difficult but also knows that reading and discussing are a waste of time unless someone actually does something. To assist, throughout the book "Change Activities" and "Applications" encourage readers to put theory into practice and do it a step at a time. He advises practical action plans for empowering others. He clarifies the methods that encourage group input to ensure that decisions are accepted and last. Importantly, he reminds leaders of the value of serving.

This book is easy to read and interesting. I encouraged you to relax, read and ponder the ideas and try the exercises. They will reminded and refresh techniques for building strong organizations and ultimately embracing the tools that great leaders use to change their world and the world of those lucky ones they lead.

—Foster W. Cline, M.D.

Dr. Cline is a well known psychiatrist and international speaker having made presentations in most states and many countries. He is the author of eight books and cofounder of the Love and Logic Institute.

ACKNOWLEDGMENT

No one makes a journey through life alone. We all owe what we learn, what we know, the skills we develop and even our lives to others. I want to acknowledge all those who have helped me learn and grow—my teachers and mentors, and especially those hundreds of people with whom I have had the privilege of working and associating—the cooks, custodians, mechanics, sales people and kids, as well as the executives and scholars—who have taught me so much and directed my view to see the real world.

I also owe much to the people who have encouraged me to share. To Dr. Foster Cline, Dr. Sally Anderson, Julie Yamamoto, my family and a number of colleagues, thanks.

Writing a book is no easy task. I appreciate the help of readers like my brother Gary, an experienced journalist who promptly threw out thirty pages of my hard work as unnecessary, Dr. Sally Anderson and Bill and Roxanne Rummler, for their comments, Brand Creative Consultant, Glenn Rummler for the book cover ideas and graphics, and critical to the final product, Stephanie Asplund and Jessica Prindle who I absolutely could not have managed without; they went page by page making comments about the mechanics as well as the ideas in the manuscript. (And yes, Jessica, we really did put men on the moon.)

Finally, a special thanks to Sally my sweet wife who has put up with and even encouraged my continual time-consuming projects and quests. It isn't easy to be married to a rubber ball that has little understanding of how to sit and relax.

Thanks to you all. I hope it was worth your efforts.

1

OVERVIEW

Why This Book

When I was in the first grade, I walked home from school with my cousin. One day at the end of school, I noticed a very small wound on my pointer finger. It did not hurt, and because it was fascinating, I wanted to share my wonderment. So, as we started walking, I pointed my finger toward his face and said, "look, blood." He immediately panicked and bolted for the door. Being caught off guard by his sudden action, I stood motionless with my finger in the air until I determined that he was heading home. I gave chase.

It mattered little how fast I walked, he sprinted ahead faster. As he ran, he cried. When he reached a crossing guard, he stopped and she pawed through his hair. When I finally caught up with him at his home, his mother was engaged in the same head searching activity and he continued to cry. What happened? Why had he run home crying all the way? And why, for goodness sakes, were people looking at his head?

As you may have already guessed, my cousin thought I was pointing at his head when I said "look, blood." Although there was no blood on his head and he felt no injury, he *perceived* there was. Because of that belief, he operated in a specific manner. In his mind, what he perceived was fact.

In the same way, what employees or members of your organization perceive will become enough of a fact to alter their actions and belief system. If they feel overlooked, left out, disenfranchised, ignored, then, in their mind, they are overlooked, left out, disenfranchised and ignored. No matter how much leadership, whether it be a board of directors, a supervisor, a principal, a superintendent, a CEO or a foreman, insists that the employee truly is a highly valued asset, if that message fails to reach the employee, the organization has dissatisfied employees.

The primary reason for this book is to convince leadership that the most important bottom line of any organization is their employees and their employees' morale, and to convince them that this message must be conveyed to those individuals in such a way that they believe it. People are not just important to the bottom line; they are the bottom line, and the greatest success in any organization will only happen when the focus is on people.

Second, and as critically important, this book provides simple exercises that facilitate the actualization of the underlying premise.

This book emerged from continual observations of thousands of situations and discussions with hundreds of people—laborers, blue-collar, semi-skilled, skilled, sales, professional—from observations of numerous enterprises, and from my experience as a leader in organizations. I hear and see the same story over and over. In the auto shop or chatting with the family doctor, in retail, wholesale, business, industry, schools, large or small organization; it does not matter. It is the feeling people have that to their leaders, they are commodities—parts—instead of important, caring, contributing, thinking human individuals.

Some leaders and organizations, aware of this concern, take action and develop policies and implement programs to be people sensitive, to utilize people input, and to provide opportunities for staff growth. Some of these have been helpful. Some have made a difference. Unfortunately, although well-meaning, many have just cost money and some have even exacerbated the problem. Many of these policies, programs and recognition practices are not perceived by the workers as authentic or helpful. In fact, some are even seen as divisive—the organization's way of attempting to placate while taking advantage.

Surprised? Perhaps not; I find some leadership awareness. Unfortunately, that view is frequently believed to be in other organizations, not in theirs. Some believe that the concern is being addressed. Others believe that regardless of approaches or management efforts, little change will ever be realized. Obviously this situation has not been resolved or human resource bookshelves would be full of knickknacks instead of books of well-meaning ideas on how to turn glazed-over apathetic robots into company cheerleaders. There are many well-written books by well-known authors. They have great advice and recommendations. However, many of these, like Senge's *The Dance of Change*, for example, require specific structures and team involvement.[1]

Overall, in my review I see good ideas, some focus and application, but not an overabundance of results—otherwise I would not keep hearing the same complaints. Like a flat tire, it matters little how many times you work on it or how much air you put in. If it does not retain the necessary profile, it is still not functional. While awareness and recognition are important and provide the first step, success requires more. This brings up the second objective and reason for this book—what to do.

This second critical objective is to help normal non-superhuman leaders convey importance to normal non-super employees and workers, and help them succeed. And through that vehicle, help the organization succeed at a greater level while getting the greatest return for the least time and money expended. Thus, this book is built on focus, application, and what I call the "hinge" principle—where a little gets a lot. To meet those criteria, success must not require significant specialized training, expensive workshops, or large commitments of time.

My approach is to focus on you and the significant changes you can make through simple steps. These will affect others and the organization incrementally. It does not require extensive sessions with staff. It is not based on the nature of your organization. It does not matter the size, service or commodity produced. It is an opportunity to try some things basically on your own. As you implement, you will create a positive and productive atmosphere that will infect—yes, infect—others.

When I worked with teachers, I saw firsthand how approaches would not work when forced, but could not be stopped when staff saw their effectiveness. A high school teacher who worked with low achieving students obtained copies of the instructional plans from other teachers, boiled them down, then taught what was important. One of the regular teachers was so amazed at the improvement in scores that he began using her approach with all of his students. A high school math teacher used a program taught in the elementary grades to help kids learn to operate more successfully with each other as well as in school and society. Other math teachers would not participate because they believed it took too much valuable math time. Our experimenting instructor made a wager that his kids would do as well or better than students in the other math classes. He won. Several other math teachers adopted the program.

People like to see success and be successful. When they see something that works, people will adopt it without pressure. This can cause a powerful chain reaction that permeates the organization and results in its greatest success.

As you read and ponder the ideas in this book, you will remember situations in your life and work that affected you and that could have been better—more productive and humane—and would have resulted in growth. Hopefully, this will add more incentive. Leaders who pay attention to the suggested principles and programs will find productivity improved, problems reduced, and profits increased. They will also enjoy their jobs more.

Who This Book is For

This book is for supervisors and foremen, for directors, superintendents and principals, for assistant managers and managers, for CEOs and board chair people. It is for those individuals who have decision-making power and positions that have impact on the people in the organization. But, by that very statement, it is easy to see how this information is also for customers, co-workers, mothers and fathers, family and friends. If you employ these principles every day in all that you do, you will have more success in all relationships.

If you are a hard-nosed, no-nonsense business person who looks at the bottom line—profit—as the evaluation of success, the content and applications in this book are critically important for you. It contains inexpensive and effective ways to increase production and cut costs, and to improve that financial bottom line. Focusing on the elements in *The Wrong Bottom Line* will produce lasting positive change. You will keep more of the best employees, even through the organization's ups and downs. You will see your workers more productive, empowered, working better together and contributing throughout the organization. You will note fewer complaints and grievances. Obviously, you will not see the end of needs or concerns—we aren't talking about magic. However, you will see better solutions created in a more peaceful atmosphere.

While this book is critically important to serious business leaders, it is also essential for school leaders and organization heads where the best is expected. The best only happens when, as Burt Nanus said, "*Leaders attract the voluntary commitment of followers, energize them, and transform organizations…*"[2] Because people are the greatest asset any organization has, and because they have the greatest capacity to contribute, the whole idea can be reduced to a simple formula: GNSP=HLOS (Greater Number of Successful People = Higher Level of Organization Success). Schools are people intensive. Thus, educators, this book will help you. The focus is on keys that maximize people; the more people you have, the greater the possibilities.

Suppose you are not a school leader, bank president, or the CEO of AT&T. What is in this book for you? Too often, we equate impact with titles. That is unfortunate; it isn't always the case.

I was once superintendent of a rather small school district. There were only four or five hundred employees. We started a tradition of having a little after-school party with each group of employees near the end of the school year. I wanted them to see that they and their contributions were important. Many of these people referred to themselves in demeaning ways. I call it the "*I'm just a*" syndrome. In talking with them I would hear: "I'm just a cook," or "I'm just a bus driver," or "I'm just a custodian." Thus, getting together over punch and cake while I listened to and talked with them was one of my efforts to help them realize their worth. I took those opportunities to thank the individuals in the group for their part in helping us make a difference to young people. I would also emphasize that there was no person or group that was deserving of the "I'm just a" designation.

Prior to one of those get-togethers with the custodians, an elementary principal asked if a fifth grade student and his parents could come to the party. He told me that they wanted to honor a custodian. Of course I approved.

In front of the group, the boy publicly thanked the custodian for his help. He related the fact that he was not always an easy child to manage. During those troubled times, the teacher allowed him to go to the one person in that school who could always work with him. From a building staff of about thirty professionals, the man who made the most difference to this boy was "just" a custodian. There were a number of moist eyes as that young man hugged his special helper, his special friend, *his special leader*.

Perhaps in your position as line worker, parent or friend, you have failed to remember how important and unique you are and how a few consistent actions will make a difference. We never know the full impact of our existence on this earth. This book is meant for you, too. It helps you better understand the human beings around you. Although some of the activities will not work for you, some will, and some could be adapted. Overall, this book presents principles, ideas, and activities that will help you be of greater assistance to the people you know.

What You Can Expect

Do, don't just read. The quicker focus turns into application, the more change will happen, and the less likely the fall-off pattern will appear. Additionally, because the applications recommended are simple, cost little or nothing, take little training, require no extensive in-services nor major philosophy pitch, yet produce exponentially, there is little reason not to do them.

Because of the complexity of work and society, and the proliferation of fairly complex philosophies, these tools and applications may seem too simple, even trite, perhaps too numerous to take the time to do. My experience has proven the opposite. I have sent individuals to very expensive workshops and training. I have reviewed many complex philosophies and ideas. Some were certainly valuable. But the things that had the most dramatic impact, the most lasting affect on the total growth and effectiveness of people and of the organization were some of the most simple. I have attempted to utilize that mode.

The Need To Focus

If you are to succeed, appropriate focus is critical. Val D. Hawks relates a story about companies awarding contracts with allowable tolerance for error. That is, they would accept the product with a percentage failure rate. But a certain foreign company awarded the contract did not understand that specification. They were confused as to why anyone would allow that deviation. After all, if it were their pacemaker or aircraft component, they did not want a defective device. In their plant, they believed in zero defects. Completely missing the point, but to comply with the specifications, they produced a number of defective parts. Dr. Hawks logically suggests that the tighter we focus on the desired outcome or target, the more likely we are to hit it.[3]

Additionally, there is a self-fulfilling prophecy component that needs to be remembered. What we believe about ourselves, others, our work, our workers, actually ensures its probability. If I believe that my employees are not very capable, are argumentative, or don't care about what they do, my actions will reflect my thinking. Those actions will convey my thinking to the workers who will tend to respond in the way I perceive them to be. That, in turn, will reinforce my belief that I was right. And, a spiral begins. As can easily be seen, this scenario can turn into a major factor in attitude and production. Dealing with union-management disputes, I often find glaring examples of this condition.

Like expert marksmen, the better we know our target, and the tighter we focus on it, the greater will be our success. Our target should be to maximize the potential of *each* and *every* individual. Focusing on a few of the chosen can at a minimum reinforce the "I'm just a…" syndrome. This can be like trying to make progress in a boat where one side is bailing like mad and the other is chopping holes. If you are lucky and skillful, you may keep the thing afloat, but progress towards the destination will be minimal.

The financial bottom line is the wrong bottom line; it is the wrong focus. In my experience, when we focus on the people—the right bottom line—all other bottom lines take care of themselves. My guarantee is that the financial bottom line will improve in step with the people bottom line.

As we started this section, let me end it. Often, we get hung up on knowledge and tied up in philosophies. It is critical to remember that it really is not what we know that affects change, it is what we do with what we know. Thus, while focus is critical, application is required.

Application and Change

Dr. Sally Anderson,[4] a consultant coaching leadership in the improvement of organizations, shared with me a problem she encounters. According to Sally, she gets lots of head-nodding and movement while she is working with people, but sees a falling away after she is gone.

What is it that keeps us from doing—applying—what we know?

First, it is more comfortable to stay where we are, do things as they have been done, and measure our progress in the same old way. We tend to see a new direction or plan with our old eyes. Thinking outside the box and moving into the unknown is scary. In business, we traditionally focus on profit-loss, market share, and gross and net sales. Education measures with attendance, seat time, state measures of average or above average scores, and meeting curriculum standards. Churches often measure success by the number of seats filled or the total in the plate. All of these standards work to a point. All of them meet some need. It is not necessarily the standards that are the problem; it is the fixation on those standards—focus problems again.

Often, we fail to realize the importance of modification. In addition to those already noted, not having a strong enough conviction of the importance of a specific change sidetracks us. In his book *Mining Group Gold*, Thomas Kayser relates how Xerox Corporation leaders realized that they must either change or go out of business.[5] Too often, it takes significant black clouds to signal eminent destruction. Unfortunately, there are numerous examples of organizations that expected the storm to blow over and the sun to shine. They failed to understand the impact of their focus, failed to do anything significant, and ultimately, failed to survive.

Tied to this is the glass-half-full catch. We don't change because we have some success in the focus we have and the way we operate. The prognosis isn't all that bad. The business is not dead. Production is acceptable. Relationships are okay. Some years back, this is what brought the American automobile industry to its knees. Fortunately, it survived. A number of others haven't been so lucky.

There is always opposition. According to Dr. Douglas L. Ratelle: "Excellence is not automatic…opposition happens constantly…prior to all of life's great victories, there comes a moment of decision…this moment is often cloudy, dark, full of a real desire to resist the truth. This moment of decision is the faithful doorkeeper of excellence. It will never accept a fraud and will reject any halfhearted attempt."[6]

Let us make a final argument for change and sum up with a statement by Mr. Kayser: "I'm convinced now, more than ever, that the one constant in the wrenching change to become a world class competitor in the global economy, the single road over which the new order of things rides, is collaboration and its facilitation within and across work teams!" He adds to that, "In the long run, how can any organization survive as a healthy, vibrant entity if it continually abuses and destroys the most valuable competitive advantage that it possesses—the collaborative brain power of its people?"[7]

An Adventure: Perspectives

This book requires leaders to view operations from a different perspective; the benefit of the workers first, and the organization second. The reasoning, tools and activities included must be used from that point of view. Nothing sours so quickly as deception close to the heart. And, as I always tell leaders, "if you are a jerk, be a jerk." Your people know that is who you are and, although they may not like it, they can certainly operate with you and have those expectations of you. However, do not expect them to operate with maximum loyalty and effort.

The exercises you are requested to do may seem contrived. In one sense, they are. They are structured. You may feel uncomfortable. That can be expected in any new adventure. Even though they are structured for you, there is no reason you cannot be sincere. Although they may seem like games, they are not. And, you will be reminded several times in this book that these cannot be considered games or devices to get what you want. They are aids to help you see from a different perspective and experience in perhaps a little different way. They are to provide a base from which you can develop additional approaches. They are focused to assist your people achieve.

This is not a "touchy feely" program. It just says that people are the most important entity in your organization. Learn to work with them from that view and you and they will be more successful. Your work will be more enjoyable. Their work will be more enjoyable. You and they will work closer to your potentials. Less time will be wasted with inconsequentials. A greater synergy will occur. Greater support will develop. And, as I have already said, if you take care of this most important bottom line—people—all other bottom lines will take care of themselves.

2

PREPARATION

Before we move on to specifics, we need to address some ideas that can help or hinder our movement. We need to come to some understandings.

First, the objective of this book is to create skills that go beyond merely the absence of problems or ways to "fix" things. The objective is to focus on developing people, and through them, more successful organizations.

Throughout this book are a number of *activities* designed to move you without fanfare or the declaration of a new "religion," into practices that are more productive. These activities are simple, not too intense, not structure-busting. They deal with the underlying reasons for disharmony, ineffectiveness, and minimal accomplishment. They are not silver bullets and will not change everything in the twinkling of an eye. However, as the underlying concerns improve, the malady will abate, and the potential of individuals will emerge. These activities have also been designed to minimize your exposure. To facilitate the steps and conserve your time, in many cases templates have been designed. The direction is consistent and the results will evolve.

While the activities are to help you become comfortable with concepts and be able to understand and use them, *applications* have been added to take the next most important step of devising strategies that actually fit your situation. Some of these will require some thinking and modifications. Because of the effort required, you may be tempted to skim through and do the activities in your mind without actually doing them, or perhaps discard them altogether. Of course, it is your choice. But while choices are yours, consequences are not. Let me explain.

We have an obesity problem in this country. Typical of the American approach, we also have a lot of remedies. Regardless, we keep gaining weight! If we continue to follow the plethora of diets and to eat as we do, that is our choice. Obviously, it has its pluses and minuses. However, like our shadow, the result—consequence—is attached. Similarly, while we certainly have the right in our organizations to make choices, we do not have the power to alter the consequences of how workers respond. I have a license to pilot an airplane. How I fly a plane is my choice. What that plane does with my input is not my choice; it is tied to the laws of physics. I used to SCUBA dive. How long I stayed at depths under the water was my choice. The consequence were I to disregard decompression charts, however, was not something I had power to manipulate.

As leaders and individuals, we have the choice to keep doing what we are doing or to modify our direction and approach. That is the only power over results we have. The Biblical observation that we reap what we sow is as true in dealing with people as it is in planting grain. While working with people is not as straightforward as the agrarian example, in my experience, the results are as constant.

Do It

Reading, thinking, dreaming, and focusing are important but make little difference in outcome unless there is another ingredient—action. Although the philosophies and practices presented in this book are grounded in centuries of thinking and personal experience, none of them will be worth much if not put into practice. Even small efforts will make a difference, but there must be effort.

Boats are turned by relatively small rudders. A small deflection makes a significant directional change. The principle is simple; the mechanism is not complex. It makes little difference to the boat, however, until the rudder is actually moved. Thus, if the path is set for a collision with a rock, another boat or some other object, discussions, admonitions or plans will make little difference; someone must activate the device. If your reading here is strictly a knowledge exercise, you are wasting your time.

This is a *do something* book. While not a workbook as such, it is a *working* book. The advice that you do not get something for nothing applies here. We all know that there are situations that seem to pay out of proportion, giving something for almost nothing—lottery winners, for example. But one has to remember that these games were not designed to benefit winners, but the organizations running them. The size of the winning amount should give us a clue to the number of non-winning contributors. The more constant payoff comes from work.

Be It

This book focuses on taking the opportunities and making the choices that tap potential. It addresses the most common and senseless waste in businesses, professions, education and organizations—people. It demonstrates how to work with people and to help them develop. It is about self-examination, about logic and common sense. It hopes to maximize success. It goes beyond doing into *being*.

Summary

After spending thousands of hours viewing organizations, listening to leaders, managers, workers of all kinds, and students in schools, it is apparent that we cling to some of the most unstable handholds while ignoring and discounting the basis for true stability and success.

The Wrong Bottom Line provides tools and techniques to locate and cling to the most stable outcroppings of hope. It then uses this new direction to optimize effort and instill the positive outlook that leads to a successful climb to the top. As in any climb, everyone is valuable. However, this is not about bonuses of turkeys, hams and checks. It is about basic values, about giving workers, employees, teachers, students, and their families the understanding that they contribute to the organization, and that it works better because of who they are and what *they* offer. A tenet is that the more one contributes, the more value he or she sees in the organization. The more value the individual sees in the organization, the greater the likelihood the organization will reach its potential.

The Wrong Bottom Line addresses the reality that businesses and institutions cling to ineffective processes even if they fail to result in optimal production. The absence of problems is neither the quest nor the same as optimal achievement. Success in *The Wrong Bottom Line* is not defined only by the lack of grievances, decreased union activity, decreased turnover, few visible signs of extensive stress, or even by test scores, profit margins or market share. Our definition of success certainly includes those indicators, but goes beyond. True success is observable by positive attitude, excitement, growth of ideas, contributions from every individual, freedom and willingness to say whatever needs to be said by anyone, ownership, eagerness to be involved, a demonstrated desire to learn and accept advice, and family support. These should be the quest. Action programs such as trust building exercises or inspirational speakers may bring momentary flashes. But, be careful, as one person put it, not to mistake the edge of the rut for the horizon. Many approaches tend to be directed *at* instead of *with and for* people, and tend not to last.

3

LEARNING

I would argue that the rate at which individuals and organizations learn may become the only sustainable competitive advantage...[8]

—Ray Stata

Recognition and honest observations by leadership are the biggest challenges I face in dealing with organizations.

To maximize our success over a period of time, we must be willing to learn. Success, as I define it, is maximizing potential, or as Peter Senge puts it in *The Fifth Discipline*,[9] the continual expansion of the capacity to create the future. Only organizations and individuals willing and aggressively pursuing an honest view of themselves and the organization, and actively doing something about it will succeed maximally.

A Key Principle of Leadership and Progress is Willingness to Learn

Regardless of everyone's desire for the perfect leader to come hurtling down on a spider web to save the day, effective leaders find themselves too often tangled in the web. A truly great leadership is marked by an intelligence that knows that he or she does not know all and cannot do everything alone. These leaders value the greatness and uniqueness of individuals, and know that we learn from each other, and are truly synergistic. One of the most rewarding parts of my experience of leadership has been chaining—experiencing the bubbling up of many ideas stimulated by listening, examining ideas, and developing new ones. As we learn, our own minds move ahead into unknown realms. Which brings us to the most essential component of success: willingness to learn.

Learner-Teacher-Learner

In this heading, "Learner-Teacher-Learner," notice that teacher is used only once and learner twice. Also, notice that the word "learner" comes before and after the word "teacher." Before you teach, learn. After you teach, learn.

Sometimes, it just seems like everyone wants to teach and share their ideas, but no one really wants to listen and learn. To grow, you must learn. To be an effective leader, you must be an effective teacher. To be an effective teacher, you must be an effective learner.

In his book *Fourth Generation Management,* Brian L. Joiner notes that if you seek rapid improvement you must seek rapid learning, and if you are in a competitive mode, you must learn and improve more rapidly than those around you.[10] I would add that only those willing to take the first step and be truly open to learning can step into the phase that Joiner believes is essential—*rapid* learning.

The brightest and best leaders I have observed realized that learning does not come just from great authorities, but from everything and everyone. In fact, they often learned the most profound concepts from observing the simplest situation or the most humble teacher. Using that model, learning and growing is not restricted by course work or workshops. The more we learn, the more unlimited our resources from which to teach since we only teach what we know. A little walk through history brings interesting sights and insights.

First, everything that has been invented, every concept that has been developed, every advancement ever made from medical practices to space exploration, and all of those discoveries that have not yet materialized, were always possible. In truth, everything—every idea, every form of transportation, every computer component—has just been waiting for someone to uncover it.

Although the early pioneers trekking across the plains were unaware, all of their wagons, belongings and livestock could have been loaded into one of today's aircraft and flown to their destinations at a speed that, in less than a minute, surpassed their normal day's journey. Those planes were possible in those days, but no one had "invented" them yet. In reality, there are no *inventions*, only discoveries and manipulation of those discoveries. Cars, trains, airplanes, even space craft were always possible. It does not matter whether we are talking communications or computers, agriculture or airplanes, philosophies or photons, all developments have always, and I repeat, *always* been there to be discovered and developed. And, although each age has tended to believe they have hit the limit, history continues to prove that belief wrong.

Second, discoveries wait for a need and/or a dreamer or astute observer, or are the result of the synergy of a group and/or the process of chaining from the ideas of others. Ideas appear to common people in common situations. An apple falling to the ground was certainly not unusual nor earth shaking, yet it meant a lot to a Mr. Newton—who no doubt had seen many such events. He just happened to be open to learning. He was an astute observer in an impressive society of discoverers—Einstein, Pasteur, Edison, Lumiere brothers, Marconi. When allowing ourselves to stand back, as it were, and really look at what is going on around us—translating ourselves from all knowing to all learning—we begin to see things we have not seen; we learn.

Similarly, when we listen to others as they present an idea, or participate in a group brainstorming session, thoughts can be generated—thoughts that would not have appeared without the comment of someone else. We learn. Learning is a decision. Before you can learn, you must decide that you will. Your challenge is to learn. You then can teach.

> Successful leaders are always learning

Pay Attention

Those who understand what is going on, must pay attention. That is not always easy.

First, *we tend to see what we expect to see.* I recall a demonstration in which people were asked to view a series of playing cards, then analyze what they saw. The cards were not normal. There was, for example, a black heart. Traditional decks do not have hearts of that color. Yet, many did not notice this or other differences because they saw what they expected to see.

I have dealt with high school students who complained that teachers called them down when they were doing "nothing wrong." In some cases the students were unaccepting of their own actions. However, in some cases they were right. These situations usually involved those who had been in trouble before and might be expected to do something inappropriate. In those cases the teachers heard a disturbance in the general vicinity of the students and automatically saw what they expected to see. In this setting, that is a problem for the less compliant student, and an advantage to children who have a reputation for being stars; they often get away with inappropriate behavior.

The boss, who you feel has always come across as a pompous know-it-all, approaches your desk. Whatever he says you are sure will be a negative put down. He says, "Good to see you at work." Your thinking goes something like this: "What do you mean see me at work! I am always at work. And, when I am at work...I work...that is more than I can say for you." The boss, however, may have noticed your contribution and been sincerely happy to see you. In contrast, in this same situation, were your best friend to make that same comment, your thinking would no doubt follow a different tack.

Second, *we sometimes just do not pay attention and we perceive through screens.* Not only do we look through our eyes and our experience, we also perceive through emotions. An employee approaches you, her supervisor, with a hostile look. The two of you have not been the best of buddies. You have a feeling of aggressiveness. Instead of the glowing "hello" you might give to some of the other workers, you hardly look up. This response does little to improve relations.

Emotions, screens, expectation, and failure to observe compromise learning. Be aware and beware.

At this point, I am about to ask you to do something. The choice you now make should give you an idea of how willing you are to learn. Bluntly, your willingness to review and attempt to use this and subsequent activities says something about your willingness to learn, and in my view, sets the parameters of your ultimate success. These activities are simple but important, as non-invasive as possible, and fun where appropriate. You might even enjoy some of them. They are designed to move you out of your current—practices cubical.

Change Activity 1

This first activity is to help you actually do something and provide a preliminary focus on how people operate.

Watch other people in your own workplace or in other businesses. It will verify what you already know: people do not treat everyone the same. It will, however, make it more apparent and illustrate ways that this treatment is manifested particularly in connection with gender.

Who Smiles and at Whom

As you observe the people around you answer the following:

1. Who smiles the most at males, men or women?
2. Who smiles the most at females, men or women?
3. When a woman is looking at other women, what does she look at?
4. When women are looking at other women, what kind of expressions do they have?
5. Do you believe these looks are merely facial or do they have an emotional connection?
6. Could this have anything to do with some events in your organization?
7. Name some.

Change Activity 2

From this small departure, observe the people you know in your organization. In the box below answer the question. (Note that throughout this book, many activities and exercises have forms. They are provided as an easy structure and encouragement for you to actually experience activities that will help you see or experience a situation, and actually begin to modify your performance, your people's performance, and ultimately the organization's performance. You do not have to write in the book. You may make as many copies of the forms as you wish. In fact, you will notice that I encourage you to involve and share, particularly with your other leaders. Also, you may wish to do an activity many times. Duplicate these as you wish. If you want to modify them, be my guest.)

1. Make a quick list of how observable countenances are affected by relationships. For example, how does the supervisor (or whomever you pick) look when he/she approaches a critic, a supervisee, a supporter, etc.? What kind of body language do you see?
2. On the right of the box note any response you see from the person(s) on the other side of that encounter or relationship.

Action	Reaction

At this point, you may be saying, "so what." A very important facet of dealing with others and in improving the job you do, regardless of what it is, is to be able to critique accurately. The more your evaluation is colored or fogged, the less you will really see, understand, and learn. Effectiveness with people comes from understanding how and why they operate as they do. While you cannot actually change others, you can change the atmosphere in which they work, and you can modify yourself. By changing yourself and the way you operate around others, they will change.

Application

Using what you have seen in the first two exercises, determine something specific related to that exercise that you can and *will* do, initiate or encourage, that will make a positive difference in your organization, family or other people. For example, you will make a conscious effort to have a pleasant look or have a positive remark every time you meet that person in the organization who you really don't like. If this is a home/family project, you might determine that the first thing you say to your spouse when you meet him or her at the end of the day will be positive—not a complaint about traffic, the dirty dishes, or the lack of money. Write what you will do on the lines below.

A warning: just like every exercise in this book, it would be very easy for you to pass over this application. After all, it seems pretty trite, of minimal importance or just busy work. So is the bottom brick in a wall. Can you imagine how much more progress could be made if the examples I just suggested were part of everyone's mode of operation? Habits change with practice; just do it.

_____

_____

_____

_____

_____

Stand Back and Look—A Fly on the Wall

Every once in a while we read about individuals who, in extreme physical distress, believed they were outside their bodies. Usually these individuals recount how they were able to see themselves as if a bystander. We are not going to get into a debate about the reality of these experiences. We can use the concept, however. And, although leadership is a demanding responsibility, it is not necessary to nearly die to learn how to observe or become exceptional. However, making yourself an observer of yourself as noted above, can certainly prove valuable in your quest to become a better leader.

Change Activity 3

Although we color the view of ourselves by strong opinions and protection mechanisms, it is still possible to observe ourselves. In this activity be aware of how you look and act, and how that changes with different individuals and in different settings. Use the following table. In the column on the left put the initials of the individual you are interacting with during your self-review. Although, these exercises are for you, as you become accustomed to what is in the book and the approaches, I suggest that you eventually get others to participate in similar exercises, No one ever has to know what you think or how you answer your questions. If you are concerned that someone will see the material and have a negative reaction, use a number or code to identify individuals instead of initials. *Be sure* you do not answer the way you think you or others think you should. The title to this book is not *How to Deceive Yourself and Others.*

Individual (initials)	How I act around this person. Were I someone observing me, what would I notice?

We have all known people who talk one way and act another—the boss who talks shared decision making but makes all the decisions, the grump who continually complains that employees don't meet customers with a cheerful countenance, the "we treat everyone the same" manager who has obvious favorites, or the "we are all equal" lady who has her own private parking spot right next to the door.

As you think on this topic, people will come to mind. As you watch those around you at work, home, or in other activities in which you are involved, you will increasingly see what I am talking about. Of course, it does not stop there. Political cartoonists feed on this aspect of leadership. In the public arena, this incongruity is continually noted.

All of this smacks of hypocrisy. And it is offensive to most people. A "do as I say, not as I do" operation is difficult to accept. When leaders *claim* they do what they say, and don't, it is a block that results in less than optimum loyalty and production. If you are a leader, check yourself.

Do you fit in this category? Are you perceived this way? These are important questions to ask. There probably could be a scale made that rates your effectiveness against the perception that others have of you. Part of the information you need can be gained from getting outside your body—being a fly on the wall. However, these visual observations can be misleading. There are other means that also need to be used.

Change Activity 4

Now for a really fun activity. Be a bit careful, however, so that you don't have people recommending you for heavy duty counseling.

1. Without being obvious, pick out an individual who you normally treat in a consistent pattern, and alter the pattern. For example, there is someone you really do not like. Someone, as you observed yourself, you notice that you tend to avoid or frown at when they are near.

2. Make it a point to stop and talk with that individual.

3. For *about three* minutes, pay attention and seriously listen (but don't look at your watch.)

    There will probably be a change in that person's reaction to you. I could eliminate the "probably" in that last statement because there *will* be a change. However, how much of a reaction and how quickly it is observable will depend on your past relationship, the length of time of the relationship, the unknown factors in the other individual, and (critical) your sincerity.

An important caution: this works as dramatically from a negative side. That is, you could interact negatively with an individual with whom you are always positive. This can be powerful enough that you can damage relationships—even if you were to explain later. Take it from my experience in this activity, *do not be negative with a person with whom you are normally positive.*

Individual (initials)	Date	Observing the reaction, what did you learn?

Application

Make the procedure above part of your weekly operation. That is, pick at least one individual and spend that time and focus that attention. Of course, this works as well at home or with students in a school setting.

Listen

Listening is another way to get information—to learn. It is also something that we usually need to work on.

We are familiar with the scenario of parents getting irritated with a teenage child who does something that he or she was told not to do, or warned against. The resultant dialogue usually contains, "you didn't listen!" In our organizations we are often guilty of the same malady.

Most of us have some blind hearing spots, as it were. We just go along at work or at home directing traffic and, as we perceive it, solving problems. This is kind of like the experience that most of us have had of putting a piece of non-assembled furniture together without reading *all* of the instructions—ultimately we get to a spot that requires us to disassemble, an action that could have been avoided if we had just "listened."

Stephen Covey in *The Seven Habits of Highly Effective People*, provides an example of how we sometimes do not listen for understanding:

A father once told me, "I can't understand my kid. He just won't listen to me at all."

"Let me restate what you just said," I replied. "You don't understand your son because he won't listen to you?"

"That's right," he replied.

"Let me try again," I said. "You don't understand your son because *he* won't listen to *you*?"

"That's what I said," he impatiently replied.

"I thought that to understand another person, *you* needed to listen to *him*," I suggested.

"Oh!" he said. There was a long pause. "Oh!" he said again, as the light began to dawn. "Oh, yeah! But I do understand him. I know what he's going through. I went through the same things myself. I guess what I don't understand is why he won't listen to me." This man didn't have the vaguest idea of what was really going on.[11]

Listening is not just hearing sound. It means that we truly pay attention and consider what is being said to us and around us, and we observe and read from an "outsider's" view. It means that we do not immediately color what we see and hear, but that we keep as open a mind as possible. It means, in the example of the cards related earlier, you would have noticed the incorrect cards. As difficult as this may be, it has big payoffs.

When you pay attention in this fashion you will be much more likely to pick up problems and take care of them before they become emergencies. For example, a CEO had an aggressive individual sitting as second in command in the organization. It was noted that this individual was spending a lot of time taking a lot of people to lunch—including the board of directors. The CEO's belief was that it was nice to have a self-motivated, aggressive member of leadership. An outside visitor remarked to the CEO that by his actions, number two was really number one. The CEO did not pay much attention to that comment. A few months later, number two *was* number one.

When you pay attention and listen, you will get more and better ideas. There are many examples of successes that were created by encouraging others to present their ideas regardless of their position. There are even more accounts of failures resulting from not paying attention. A retail chain had a practice of laying off many of their workers during a slower time of year. Some of those people never came back when the rehiring started again. The result was that more time and money had to be spent finding, hiring and training new recruits. Additionally, trainees are seldom as effective as seasoned workers. A night stock manager observed that during this same slow time, the corporate office continued to send large quantities of merchandise months before they were needed. Those commodities eventually became hard to manage, had to be sorted, stored and resorted. In addition to keeping an expensive inventory, the worker hours required to handle this problem added to the costs. This manager believed the company would actually save money if they would slow down the buying and storing which created the continual waste of employee hours moving the merchandise, and use the money to maintain their employees. Management never listened. So, they are still trying to find more space for back room stocking while they go through the costly and unpleasant task of firing, hiring and training. And, by the way, that manager left that group.

A consultant noted that in situation after situation with which she deals, the workers believe that management always blames them when things go wrong, won't give them the authority to change the process, and won't listen to their ideas to make the system work. As leaders and managers we do not have all of the answers. It is dangerous to believe we do.

When you pay attention and listen, you will create a team feeling and dedication that will reach a magnitude not possible any other way. A loyalty to you and the organization will occur that will affect statistics and will go beyond measurement. Of course, this holds true of the treatment of customers. Truly listening and showing that you really do regard people as intelligent and important individuals will pay big dividends. If you pay attention to only a few things in this book, *listening* should be one you choose.

Change Activity 5 and Application

1. Set aside a time to listen. Determine who you will listen to. Determine that during the listening time, you will pay attention—at least 100%. You will not let your mind wander. You will mentally note the ideas.

2. Determine within your own mind when you will return and comment to the individual to whom you are listening, regarding your session. Don't tell the person that you are doing an exercise. Don't schedule a time with the individual when you will come back. At a later time, just stop by and comment about some remark or idea that came from the original meeting. Notice the affect on you and on the other person.

Individual (initials)	Listening date	Ideas to note	Stop by date	Observations

Important Reminder: These exercises may seem trite and like a game. **These are not part of a game.** You may think that it is a frill or a waste of time. It is neither. The literally thousands of individuals with whom I have talked and/or observed have verified—repeatedly verified—the importance of what I am recommending. You may also believe that you do this all of the time. Unless you are an individual with few flaws, there is *someone* to whom you have not listened, particularly, someone you don't like. *Go back to the activities and do them.*

Although these exercises will make an immediate impact on others, they are for <u>you</u>. If you are unwilling to spend this minimum time and minor effort to give them a try, that should give you a clue about you. You may want to consider that carefully. Later, I will be providing a systematic approach that has much more impact than these simple exercises. However, these exercises may prove more enlightening and show more positive results than you imagined.

4

LOGICAL THINKING

The organizations that will truly excel in the future will be the organizations that discover how to tap people's commitment and capacity to learn at all levels in an organization.[12]

—Peter Senge

Logical thinking, or what used to be called common sense, can play an important part in your progress toward focusing on the most productive bottom line—maximization of human potential—and making lasting change. Logical thinking is a basic mode of thinking, of looking at where we are and how we operate. The absence of this common sense approach causes considerable stress and unnecessary problems in our organizations and in our lives. As we view others, not operating in a logical way sticks out like the proverbial sore thumb. Yet, when inferred that our operations or mode of functioning are not logical, we deny the malady.

A woman, whose car ran into the back of the one ahead explained to the policeman that a donut sitting on the seat next to her rolled to the floor; she leaned over to pick it up. A man standing beside his car with a flat tire kicked the tire and hurt his foot. A woman stuck her finger into the grass chute of the running rotary lawn mower and cut the tip. A man clearing the snow from his driveway tried to clear the auger of his snowblower while it was running, and lost fingers in the process. An angry young man smashed his doubled fist into a concrete wall, resulting in pain and broken bones. These actual events are not news. These are common occurrences in normal everyday life that illustrate how we often drift away from the obvious.

You know individuals who did something that did not seem to be a very good idea. You have read articles in the newspaper or seen situations reported on television that went against "smart" thinking. Perhaps, even you have done something (or a number of things) that you have decided were really "dumb"! A high school shop teacher who spent considerable time with his students stressing safety, during class cut off the end of his finger with a table saw. He muttered more about the stupidity he felt than the actual pain from the wound. He had been distracted by students and had let his eyes leave the job at hand—something he continually warned his students not to do.

Examples are found in business, education, organizations of all kinds, and in everyday living; the world is full of them. Particularly in the people aspect of your organization, not maintaining a practical view—common sense—can be extremely distressing and costly to your organization.

Assuming you would like to void some missteps and increase productivity by using more common sense or logical thinking, let us look at a couple of keys.

Think Ahead

One of the ways to develop better thinking and operating patterns is to look at the possible results. Granted, that is not always easy to do in every situation. Working at developing a habit of imagining or forecasting outcomes will benefit you and your organization. Like the old recommendation to count to ten before acting, it makes you stop and think instead of just acting or reacting. Particularly bad examples are all around us.

My wife and I were sitting in a fairly expensive restaurant. A couple at a nearby table had been seated for some time. Waiters had passed them by. Finally, these patrons became upset and shared their feelings with a passing server. Their complaint was noted to the manager. She came forward. The couple lamented that they had been waiting for twenty minutes without service. The manager, much to our surprise, took the stance that it had only been fifteen minutes! An argument ensued ending in the couple getting up and leaving. The appropriate scenario is so obvious that, in my use of it in teaching mock interviews to many, many people, no one has ever offered the solution taken by the manager. It is absolutely void of common sense. By the way, that business is no longer in operation.

Often, pride gets in the way of intelligent thinking. In another restaurant, a customer became somewhat demanding and unpleasant. The waitress returned that demeanor. Throughout the meal, the situation accelerated until no one enjoyed the meal and the others in the party were weary of the obvious hostility. Neither the waitress nor the customer won. In fact they both lost—the waitress with no tip, and the customer with belligerent and minimal service.

A business owner who was having problems with computer software, called the company for assistance. The response was that since they had marketed an update of that particular product, they would not respond to questions regarding previous versions. The owner explained to the representative that he understood that the software company would be training their people on the newest software, but that there should be someone who could help him with his problem. After all, his version was not that old, and there would likely be tech people who would know how to fix it. His request was denied. They suggested he purchase the updated version. The result was a letter written to that company by the software owner, informing them that his organization would not be buying the new update nor any other material from them in the future. The producer never responded.

Perhaps by now, you are growing weary of examples that seem almost ridiculous. Sadly, they represent hundreds. I constantly see them in organization after organization. You can probably stop strangers on the street and they will share similar things about their place of work or about those they have dealt with. Too often, these situations are like our noses—we don't see them, but everyone else does.

The point is that in these actions, somehow, in some way, the obviously correct choice just did not happen. It was somehow overlooked or ignored. When the logical action was known and seemed so obvious, why would anyone do anything else? Of course, as in all actions, there are reasons. Often, someone was not considering the big picture; they were not thinking ahead.

Becoming more observant and acting appropriately are skills that can get better with practice. That leads us to activity six.

Change Activity 6

Since what we have just reviewed are not isolated moments in history, since they happen to all of us on a frequent basis, and since they create all kinds of problems, take a minute, step off the merry-go-round, and look around.

1.   Review the organization, home, the news, or life in general.

2.   Identify at least one situation that did not seem logical to you.

3.   Determine a better course of action.

Event or Situation	What was seemingly not logical?	What should have been done?

Application

It is better to determine logical thinking ahead of a situation. Review an upcoming event. See if there are things that could be more logical. Do a simple one. For example, often at workshops and conventions heavy lunches are served. These are accompanied by long speeches and followed by more workshops or presentations. What problems does this cause? What can you come up with that is more productive?

Perspective

In the situations listed and the ones you noted, something was amiss. Too often, instead of just being analysts, however, we become negative critics. Not only is that not helpful to those we criticize and to us, it is not necessary. Sometimes we ridicule the organization or the people involved because it seems to us that someone could have made better choices, enacted more intelligent procedures, or used some common sense in developing policy. If we want to optimize, if we want to be successful, it is important for us to recognize these unproductive situations. However, blaming and criticizing does not add anything; as one individual put it, when you are throwing mud, you are losing ground. We are here to learn so that we can improve, so that we can minimize the less effective and maximize the more effective.

There are reasons behind all actions. Thus, our first focus is on trying to discover what would precipitate these obviously illogical non-productive activities. Let us explore some possibilities. Perhaps it will help you avoid unnecessary criticism and possible future problems.

First, *some things are not as apparent as they seem*—particularly from some views and in some situations. Sometimes, from our vantage point, we just do not see clearly. Sometimes we refuse to perceive the obvious—we push it out of our sight. Standing from the outside, a different plan may seem obvious. However, the person enmeshed may not see what someone less involved sees. Emotion, habit, advice, tradition, rapidness of events, tight timelines and many other factors cloud the way individuals operate in any given event. Thus, in the heat of the situation—the young man slamming his hand into the concrete, the woman sticking her finger into the moving blade—the mind was just not focused on the reality of the action. Although the individuals were aware of the damage possibility, it was not glaringly apparent enough to result in a different action.

It is said that Ben Franklin always waited three days before mailing critical letters. As a result of looking at them from a delayed perspective, he almost always decided not to send them.

Second, *ignorance influences our perspective.* Ignorance can be defined in a number of ways. Not understanding one or more of the principles involved, lack of perspective of related factors such as emotions and relationships, and just plain lack of general information all play in the dynamics that affect situations. The CEO wanted to improve personal communications, so he added assistants to free time for his involvement. However, in so doing, he actually added another layer of insulation between himself and the workers. The result was exactly the opposite of his goal. Although his free time allowed him to visit personally with some folks, overall his actions created a feeling by most workers of greater distance. Also, because he found himself with additional time, it quickly filled with other things.

In a presentation to a group of people, one may not realize the backgrounds, experience or mindset of the gathering. I was once asked to provide balance to a presentation by addressing one side of an issue. Because I knew that it was a touchy topic and I would be taking the unpopular side, I prepared a logic that I felt would be absolutely obvious to anyone. During the presentation, as I applied my logic, I became aware of an almost vacant stare in the eyes of those in attendance. Their thinking was so focused on the other view that they virtually did not hear what I was saying! I was unprepared and ignorant of the depth of their predisposed position.

It is good common sense to learn as much as possible about the group, institution, individuals and situations with which you plan to work so that ignorance does not rule the action.

Third, *applicability to me and my situation.* Advice is always easy to find. Platitudes are on every wall. But do they really apply to me or my organization? Things are going quite well. Profits are up. Is a different approach really necessary? And, will it really work in "my" situation? Although experience verifies that some things do work, there are situations where the best advice, the most logical approach or the most obvious solutions do not seem to pay. Does this action really apply to me and my organization, and at this time? Do we really want to take the chance of making a change?

The CEO of a significant company with whom I spoke, voiced his understanding that probably what I was proposing could be of value. He also noted that he had seen where this approach had made a very significant improvement in another organization. But things were going quite well in his business, so…. The unfortunate side of that kind of thinking is illustrated by the dead seat belt procrastinator, the cancer infected smoker, and the life jacket-less drowning victim. All were aware of the dangers. All were willing to take the steps if and when danger was eminent. All died because once started, the events moved too fast to allow the change. The time to improve the company is when it is stable, not just before it crashes. Which brings us to the next reason.

Fourth, *hang on because things will get better.* There is a tendency to stay with what we know or with what we feel comfortable. One of the most compelling reasons for major problems experienced by United States businesses a few years back was directly connected to the propensity to stay with what worked in the past. And, it continues to be a danger.

As can be demonstrated in many situations, this mind set can make it almost impossible for us to move to a new pattern or solution. We actually become blind to solutions because of our traditional way of viewing them. Additionally, as I have already noted, sometimes a little success is worse than a heavy loss. It is enough to feed the belief that the best solution is tied to just doing what is being done, only more intensely, a little bit better, a little longer, or tweaking some facet. Although this works in some cases, it is important to remember a sage phrase: "When the horse is dead, it is time to dismount." Sometimes, we fail to accurately appraise the health of the animal and/or follow the advice. We keep tweaking the creature—moving the limbs, loosening the bridle, yelling commands and remembering that it did work just a little while ago. When things do not seem to be going well, many businesses stay with the original design while reworking the product or changing the color or size only to find that it does not improve the situation.

This seems to be kind of a built-in factor. Considerable research illustrates the very strong tendency for an organism to stay with what has brought past success even though it is obvious that it will not work. In fact, one of Newton's laws of motion applies. In operant conditioning studies, the Skinnerian rat experiment using a charged grid and an escape door illustrated that even after the escape door was closed, the rat kept jumping into it. In your own physical body, you may have noticed this tendency. As you attempt to lose weight, you eat all the right foods, do all the exercises, and follow all of the plan, yet the numbers on the scale just keep bouncing back to where they were!

When television first appeared, many motion picture theaters continued in the same traditional ways. They had one screen and one projectionist who had to be with the projection machines to change, thread, and rewind reels every five to twenty minutes, make manual coordinated changeovers between machines and see that the carbon arcs were kept lit and maintained to provide light during the performances. And the candy and popcorn cost the same reasonable price you paid at the local grocery store. Having grown up in that business, I watched the family theaters shrink in number and then slip into extinction. This process took several years. Always the hope of my father was that continuing as he always had—providing excellent service at a reasonable price—would win the day. It didn't.

After a short time, logical thinking would dictate that what was being done was not working, and that changes needed to be made. At that time, the trends were steadily moving away from the success of small theaters. To bring movies back and make them work, it took someone changing the way theaters were operated—one projectionist for several grouped auditoriums, continuous film feed machines, self-sustaining light sources, and prices at the candy counter that were excessive. That and other changes in perspective brought movie theaters back more plentifully than ever. Unfortunately, my father hung on and hung on in the old way until he lost not only the business, but his own financial safety. Staying with what was known and comfortable ultimately resulted in the greatest discomfort.

Fifth, *common sense principles are viewed as too easy, simple and inexpensive.* Sometimes we reason that complex situations require complex remedies. Sometimes they do. But sometimes they do not. I recall the advice that you pay for what you get. Although this principle should remain in plain view, it is wise not to automatically discard more simple and often cheaper paths. If you are not careful, sometimes you pay for *more* than you get. Solutions do not always take great brilliant minds or college degrees. Even great skill is not always necessary. Sometimes, the most simple approach is the best solution. When the United States was attempting to get its first satellite into orbit, all kinds of highbred rockets were tried. How well I remember getting up in the early hours, turning on the television, waiting through the long countdowns, and then watching the massive fire shows and explosions as time after time rockets failed to get where they were meant to go. Eventually, common sense and a straight-forward approach prevailed. Success came in the form of a modified World War II rocket—nothing fancy; it was just reliable. It got the job done.

A good rule here is to go from the simple to the complex. The solution may not take an earth-shattering idea or a major modification. Simple may be better. Of course, we have to look out for staying with comfort or not applying intelligent thinking.

Summary

We go through life thinking "it" will not happen to me. We probably do that as a way to keep our sanity. Obviously, if from the moment we woke up until the last flicker of thought before falling asleep at night, we thought of all the possible problems that could befall us, we would not be able to manage life. The flip side of that coin, however, is going through life with our heads in the sand, so to speak, believing that we can ignore the "danger" and "caution" signs. September 11 stands as a stark reality of the unimaginable happening. The absolute absurdity that a plane could and would be high-jacked and flown into a prominent building in New York, though broached with officials, was too unthinkable to address. The fact that <u>three</u> airliners were successfully high-jacked on the same day and successfully crashed into three different buildings was beyond possibility. The results were shattering to those in the planes and the buildings. They also forever impacted billions of people across the world, and testified that the unbelievable can and does happen.

The lady with the donut knew that when operating a moving vehicle in traffic, it was unwise to lean down and pick something off the floor. Were there a law of practice that said, "every time you lean over and reach for something on the other side of the car, you will wreck," she would not have attempted to pick up the donut. She didn't believe *she* would get into a wreck by leaning over *this* time.

Because our actions do not *always* reap a negative result and we seem to get away with some practices, we consciously or unconsciously believe it will continue time after time. There is usually some small part of the equation that allows us to skim by sometimes without bad consequences. But like the old game of Russian Roulette, eventually a loaded chamber will appear. A father who instructed his son to break a rule of hunting and disengage the safety on his rifle while they were approaching game ahead, was killed by the bullet accidentally discharged. The pilot who was having fun dropping bags of flour near a boy scout troop, forgot the rules of handling his aircraft and the laws of physics, and flew too low and slow. It ended with a tragic crash that will long be remembered by his young scouting friends.

In the world of organizations, education, or families, the results are not always so dramatic and tragic. However, they are just as real and effecting. Treating employees and customers with indifference, providing less than optimal quality or service, or failing to improve during good times, all have the same ultimate affect. Previous positive experiences can actually prove to be one of our worst enemies. Too often in related circumstances, no noted negative results happened.

The lady in the wreck had probably at some time or other, while driving a car, reached for something near her with no negative affects. The father had probably taken the safety off his gun while walking through the woods at some time without tragedy. The pilot had probably flown the plane in a somewhat similar configuration and not crashed. In each of these, however, a different element was present. It may have been very slight, almost imperceptible, yet it was enough to make the difference.

A complication of this idea is that these negative consequences have generally not happened *yet*. As noted above, however, that does not lessen the consequences. For example, the medical community has connected irrefutable evidence to the hazards of smoking. But everyone who smokes does not immediately have complications nor do they all die from smoking related diseases. This lulls tobacco users into a mindset that statistically has a good chance of a less then happy ending. Similarly, the organization has always been able to work through its problems. The market has always supported the industry. The workers have usually been happy.

Be careful. Just because it has not happened, does not mean it won't.

Change Activity 7

1. Go back and review the situations you noted in *Activity 6*.

2. Do a little analysis and determine which of the reasons listed in this chapter probably applied.

3. Note the reasons in the margin next to the incident.

There are many reasons why logical reasoning is not common enough. And it is not the only answer in maximizing the potential of your people or in solving every problem. However, it should be a departure point. It should be the first thought to stimulate questions that need to be asked: What is going on here? Why is everyone acting as they are? Is this the most straightforward approach? Is this the best approach? Are there things that are apparent to which I am not paying attention? What do I know that I am not applying?

This is also applicable to the examination of larger decisions like those that seem to follow current trends. Making best choices obviously can and should be assisted by looking at the philosophy behind the idea, the logistics required to make it work, the possible long-term advantage, costs, staff acceptance or concerns overall, and the total logicalness of the step.

The catch point here is that while most organizations do use a logical process in making large decisions, they often overlook what they perceive as insignificant ones. Too often, these deal with everyday, people-affecting operations and policies. In reality, these "inconsequential" concerns can ultimately impact their operation most significantly.

Common sense is not exclusive; it is the right of everyone. You do not need a degree or a certificate to use it. In the process of determining your plan of action or response, be careful not to let some of the common sense blockers keep you from finding the most simple, most productive, and best plan of action.

Change Activity 8

Particularly after poor decisions, we often hear the phrase that hind sight is 20/20. Of course, that means that better decisions could have been made had we been able to see the outcome. No one makes all the best decisions, but sometimes we maintain thinking and/or conditions that set us up, as it were, and will result in less productive decisions.

1. Review some current practices or processes in your organization.

2. Attempt to analyze it to the point of determining why they were implemented that way.

3.   Note logical thinking alterations that would improve the operation.

4.   Select at least one that you have some power to alter, and set a time line for alteration.

Situation	Why implemented	Alteration for improvement	Date to begin change

Change Activity 9

We are going to call this activity "through other's eyes." We have talked about how strange, even irrational, some actions and responses seem. Activity 8, which you should have completed, is all from *your* perspective. This is necessary, of course. But now, let us get some other opinions.

Listening to others is one of the themes of this book for a very sound reason. There is no way you can see all things in all ways. If you are in a business, you review graphs and reports. They can provide considerable information. What they do not provide so well are such things as ideas and staff potential. The more views you have, the more you will see and understand the situation and the people, and the greater possibility that you will make the most effective and productive decisions. Unfortunately, too often I find leadership not interested. Some of them do not want to know what their people think. Others are concerned they are turning the operation over to the "regulars," the rank and file folks. This insecurity can be minimized if you only remember that you are just gathering information and input; the final decisions can still be made by leadership. My personal experience is that the willingness and practice of asking for the views of others is one of the best predictors of success.

1.   Make copies of the form (change activity 8). Keep the same areas, situations, policies, etc.

2.   Give it to a few individuals with whom you work. Have them evaluate as you did.

3. If this is the first time you have done something like this, or if you are concerned that they do not trust you and may answer to protect their jobs, set up a secretary or someone to receive the forms and, perhaps, even summarize them.

4. Compare your opinions with the responses from others.

5. In a meeting with all of them, acknowledge some of the recommendations they provided and, if possible, announce an implementation time for one.

If you pay attention to their opinions and actually use them to color some of your final decisions, you will find them willing to tell you more, and to do so openly. You will just have added a number of extra eyes and brains.

A caution here: sometimes I find what appears to be almost complete agreement of the group with the leader. Although this can certainly be a reality, it can also be a red flag that indicates a lack of trust by the employees. Few people are willing to grease the guillotine for their own necks. You must be extremely sincere and must illustrate that; there can be absolutely no belittling or repercussions.

5

UNDERSTANDING YOUR ROLE

There are plenty of excellent *managers* in organizations—people who meet schedules, control budgets, develop plans, or coordinate the efforts of subordinates to provide a service or product. But *leadership* is another thing entirely…Leaders attract the voluntary commitment of followers, energize them, and transform organizations.[13]

—Burt Nanus

Setting a New Profile

Leaders are not always held in high regard. In fact, often in our society, we treat leaders negatively. We criticize the supervisors, blame the bosses, vilify the CEOs, and make fun of the President. Unfortunately, too many individuals in these roles have provided ample material with which we can work. Your job as a leader is to establish a different profile. Robert Greenleaf in *Servant Leadership*[14] sees leaders as not only prime movers, but also servants. He places leaders as those who are saviors of people and institutions.

Learning and effective leadership are closely connected. Learning leaders are critically important. John Kennedy stated that leadership and learning are indispensable to each other.[15] Peter Senge notes in *The Fifth Discipline* that in learning organizations, leaders are important designers, stewards and teachers.[16] Stephen Covey in his *The 7 Habits of Highly Effective People*[17] notes that leaders radiate positive energy and are continually learning.

It is unnecessary to go on. We have all noted the significant positive affect or the devastating negative consequences of leadership. And we have ample examples of leaders who needed to learn. So let us move on and take a closer look at leadership.

There Are Always Leaders

Although there have always been leaders, there are now leaders, and there will always be leaders in the future, they are not necessarily the obvious ones. We see the elections and note the chairpeople and the candidates. We observe the town meetings, and we see the city councils and the mayors. The armed services come with generals, captains, lieutenants and so on. The fire department and the police follow suit. Jobs come with CEOs, vice-presidents and supervisors. Boards of directors have chair people. Bosses seem to be everywhere. There is even a spokesperson for the group protest. While in the usual definition these are all leaders, the actual power varies. Their influence also varies from strong follower-ship to grudging servitude or even rebellion.

Leadership often comes with education, experience, money and position. It comes with insignias and name plates, uniforms and even parking spots. But leaders do not have to be appointed, although they might. They do not have to earn more money and benefits, although they usually do. They do not have to hold higher degree, yet some do. They do not always have more experience, but it is often the case. Certainly, you will find leaders fitting some or even all of these descriptions. However, actual leadership does not always go with this list.

There are leaders who hold official positions. There are also those leaders who lead but have no formal designation. In fact, sometimes a problem is created when the people follow an individual *other than* the titled leader.

Stop what you are doing. Look out the window. Find a group of kids and watch their interactions. You will see leaders. here was no election, no appointment, no training. Watch the people on the street or at work. You will see leaders without appointments or official recognition. Even the ducks at the park have leaders. There have always been leaders. There will always be leaders. The accumulation of degrees, experience or insignias may indicate leadership, or merely position. All of these do not ensure the kind of leadership that maximizes people potential.

The Misunderstood Role

Leaders play the most significant and critical role in the development of people and the ultimate success or failure of the organization.

An individual with whom I worked once asked if I knew why the lead goose in a flock was the leader. This individual had a ready wit, and this question could be assumed to have a funny or pun ending. Rather than make a lot of guesses that would probably be in error, I said, "I don't know." He answered, "because the other geese are following!" At first, that seemed like a typical groaner. However, as I thought about it, I began to understand the significant wisdom in that statement. Leadership *is* more than a spot in the formation, or a title or slot on an organization chart. True leadership is identified by follower-ship. A human leader, just like the lead goose, breaks the ground (air) in front and makes it easier for the rest of the flock. Human leaders also set the pace and the direction.

If you find the group straying and determining to push off without you, it is time for a careful check— if they are not following, you are not leading.

If They Are Not Following, You Are Not Leading

Numerous books have been written discussing leadership. Some classify leaders into styles. You may have done a test or two. It may have involved a matrix with your style being pegged into one quadrant or another. Perhaps, after reviewing some of this literature, the whole idea may seem too complex, confusing, and not worth the effort. After all, good leaders use seven principles, mind their minutes, put first things first, provide a learning environment, are designers, have vision, are passionately committed, recognize the value of people, are excellent communicators, manage from the left side of the brain and lead from the right, are continually self-improving, are searching for excellence, and leap tall buildings with a single bound. Maybe, after submersion in all of the material, being a good leader may seem more impossible than ever. Or, it may seem like the whole issue is a bit overdone and unnecessary—maybe even a waste of time.

Leadership, like good listening, is often misunderstood. In effective listening, the advice often centers on posture, eye contact, ability to use reflection and so on. However, the way to truly gauge effective listening is not through what the listener does, but what transpires around the *teller*. Good listeners find themselves surrounded by people who want to talk. Thus, if people seek you out to share with you, you are a good listener. And, although you are probably doing many of the things identified as good listener practices, frankly, if you stand on your head in the corner yet people line up to talk to you, you are a good listener. On the other hand, if no one ever confides in you, you probably do not score very high as a listener.

Likewise, *good leaders are identifiable by the number of people who willingly choose to follow them.* All of the other things are purely academic. I have witnessed supposed leaders who appeared to possess and exhibit the right traits and actions, yet whose followers were there only because they were compelled to be, and had little but negative things to say about their chief.

> **Leadership is not a goal to attain as much as a process to develop.**

Leadership is not a goal to attain as much as a process to develop. The first step is to continually be awake and aware, and be willing to learn and improve. With that as the foundation, you will become a better leader. You will also have the first step in making the greatest positive difference in the people and situations with which you work.

Reading books and reviewing styles and procedures of good leaders and effective operations is certainly not a bad move. There is much information to be acquired. Other resources can assist you in better seeing what kind of leadership style you use most often. Self examination is helpful. If you read, study and view yourself using all of the many materials out there—and with an attitude of learning—you will benefit. However, don't forget that *your* benefit is not what leadership is all about. All of this is worth nothing to the people or organization unless it affects your attitude and actions—and I cannot emphasize that enough. Your effectiveness as a leader is directly connected to your attitude and the actions that illustrate that attitude.

> **Your effectiveness as a leader is directly connected to your attitude and actions that illustrate that attitude.**

Although leadership *may* come dressed in degrees, training, experience, or position, we have all seen people with both who were not leaders. They may have held the coveted position.

They may have even had the power to require submission, may have been managers or administrators, but they were not leaders. The true test of leadership is the power manifest when it is not required or coerced. The true test of leadership is manifest not by the power *demanded*, but the power willingly *given* by followers.

> **Successful leaders have successful followers…and successful followers have successful leaders.**

Improving Leadership

As you will recall, my commitment in this book is three-fold: (1) not to spend your time on endless philosophy, (2) not to burden you with extensive and elaborate individual or organizational alterations that take time, money and retooling, and (3) to provide simple exercises that will, step by step, get you to modify your approach and ultimately the atmosphere of your organization. The expectation is that you will see results immediately and desire to move in the direction in which the exercise focuses. Hopefully, this will also foster ideas that will motivate you to begin developing procedures and practices that you can share with your leadership and that are more specifically tailored to the needs of your organization.

Before we go on, however, let us examine a base for overall organization improvement: atmosphere.

I define atmosphere as the permeating feeling within any organization. A productive atmosphere is the critical ingredient in the maximization of potential. Atmosphere is tied to what is perceived as the observable vision of leadership. Its effectiveness is in close ratio to the congruency of what is said when measured against what is done. As Naisbitt and Aburdene noted in *Re-inventing the Corporation*, "The only way to translate vision and alignment into people's day-to-day behavior is by grounding these lofty concepts in the company's day-to-day environment."[18]

Change Activity 10

Because we sometimes miss the real leaders in the group—the people who others actually follow most readily—let us run a kind of sociogram.

1. Distribute copies of the questionnaire that follows.
2. If there are fewer than 12 individuals who would seem to be considered by the workers as leaders or helpers, still leave all the blanks. It encourages your people to think outside the most obvious. You may discover some possibilities of which you were unaware. Although you can put more than 12 slots, you are not likely to benefit much since most people will not even complete that number. If they have more, just have them add to the chart.

3.   Although this information will be more helpful if individuals completing it will indicate their names, it can be done anonymously. The biggest advantage of having names of those completing the forms attached to the forms is in developing teams; you find who will work best with different leaders. However, a bigger down side is that the individuals may complete it as they feel they should—a more politically correct spin that will give you nothing to work from.

To help us be more helpful in assisting you and in developing effective teams, please, *list in order* who you would go to for leadership, guidance, and direction. These individuals do not have to be part of your group or department. They also do not have to be designated heads or serving in a leadership role.

Individual's name	Individual's current position
1.	
2.	
3.	
4.	
5.	
6.	
7.	
8.	
9.	
10.	
11.	
12.	

Leadership Sociogram

To make some sense of the lists you have just received and to get a more clear view of leadership do the following:

1. On a sheet of paper, in a random pattern (don't line them up) place the name, initials or code name of each individual completing this form.
2. Next, place the name or initials of the first choice of each individual on the sheet.
3. Using a red pen, pencil or marker, draw a line between the chooser and the chosen.
4. Put an arrowhead on the end of the line that indicates the person chosen.

After you have gone through all of the number one choices indicated by all of the participants, you should have a pattern of who the leaders are. On this same sheet, using a blue pen, pencil or marker, connect the second choices. You may wish to go further down the list using different colors. The limitation to this system is how honest your people dare to be. Unfortunately, in some organizations individuals suffer negative consequences for candid information. If the responses of your people in all sections of your organization look like your organizational chart, that could be a red flag.

Application

Now for the acid test. If you truly want to be a better leader, if you sincerely want to improve the organization and develop and optimize the potential of people, you have to be willing to look at you and the way you operate through *their* eyes. Sophisticated tools are not necessary. Expensive consultants are not required; put the checkbook back in the drawer. The best way to find out how people view you is to ask them. The only problem we have in this exercise is to assure *them* that (1) you sincerely want their input, (2) you will use it where possible, and (3) their positions, jobs, or relationships are not in danger should you not like what they say. The following is a template which may be used and should minimize their fears.

Change Activity 11

Your Opinion Please

In an effort to make the organization [company name, business, group, etc.] better, more effective, and to assist you and me to do our part in the most positive and accommodating way, I need everyone's help. This is totally anonymous. But because I want to hear from everyone, I am asking you to please check off your name as you place the questionnaire in the box provided. They will be compiled by [secretary, clerical, etc]. Thank you.

Please:

1.   Complete this questionnaire honestly and accurately; I sincerely want your candid input.
2.   Do not sign it.
3.   Fold it and tape or staple it closed.
4.   Deposit it in the box [secretary's desk, etc.] by [date].
5.   Check your name off the list.

Things I like about [organization name]:
Things I would like to see changed about [organization name]:
Things I like about [your name]:
Things I would like to see you change about you and the way you operate:
Other comments:

Follow Up

Your three objectives in the exercise were to (1) get people to express themselves honestly, (2) gain information, and (3) implement a step for trust. I emphasize the end of that statement—for trust. While implementing good ideas from staff is important, developing their trust in you and the fact that you truly do want their input, is most critical. With this in mind, there are two things you must guard against. First, regardless of what is said or who says it, you must not retaliate in *any* way. I emphasize *any* because some people may not trust you and will be looking for a negative move on your part. Because of the comments you may get, you may have an idea of who wrote what. Do not show any indication of knowing. You can only build trust by being trustworthy. One of the points made by Senge in *The Dance of Change*[19] is that people have to learn to feel safe if they are expected to contribute.

A CEO I knew was outgoing, friendly, personable, and seemed very interested in his people's opinions and well-being. However, those who expressed their true beliefs and feelings about him or the organization found themselves in negative locations and working on assignments for which they were not well trained. The message sent was to keep quiet or suffer the consequences of failure and eventual dismissal. Obviously, it would have been better had this individual not put forth this facade. As I will keep repeating: if you are a jerk, be a jerk; it works better.

The second objective was to gain information. If this is a new experience for the staff, and if they have had bad experiences either with you or with some other leader, the first information will be pretty benign because they are testing the water. In the case above, the information was of little value. No one wants to put a lot of thought and effort into an exercise that is just that, an exercise, and could be detrimental to their situation. However, if you as their leader actually acknowledges the information gained by sharing it or acting on it, subsequent questionnaires will gain more and more accurate information. In fact, a good tactic is to select a couple of the prominent or reoccurring comments and put out a short questionnaire asking for additional information. If the staff is open, a better approach is to bring the idea up in a meeting for further discussion.

Make sure that these exercises are not just busy work. Everyone has plenty to do without playing games with leaders.

Third, if your workers deem you trustworthy they will begin to go out of their way to share. Not only will that provide more eyes, as it were, to assist you in forming the most accurate picture of what is going on, it will also begin to create communication, positive beliefs about the organization and a greater commitment to you and the business. Benefits become exponential—the more involved they are, the quicker problems are noticed and productive ideas contributed. They become more supportive of you and more forgiving of your mistakes. They take responsibility for making the organization succeed. They feel it a part of them—turnover is reduced. And so on and so on.

Since there are always leaders, and since leaders possess the greatest opportunity for developing the most important bottom line—people—it is critically important that leaders understand and pay attention to some basic common sense principles. I again emphasize that knowledge is worthless unless it affects application. Gasoline is merely a cold, smelly liquid until a spark ignites its potential.

Leadership Changes Lives

Leadership is a privilege that allows us to have a greater positive impact on the lives of human beings. No, you will not find that definition in the dictionary, unfortunately. From my experience and observations, however, I am convinced that if this were the prevailing doctrine, there would be more successful organizations, and organizations that were more successful. There would be found within each business greater human resources and a more positive, exciting and productive atmosphere. Assuming that my statement is correct and that this definition and way of thinking are the most productive, why is it not the basis for operation in all institutions?

Let me accept responsibility for the statement by first stating that anyone who has reviewed even commonly known and demonstrated ideas about leadership have to notice a philosophy based on the value of facilitating the development and cooperation of people. In fact, logical thinking tells us that any organizations that espouse a divergent philosophy will never be optimally successful. Business and institutional attention to net profit, market share, goal acquisition, return ratios, and statistical analysis are appropriate and necessary. Unfortunately, too often those components become the focus instead of the measurement. If the focus is on facilitating the growth of people and improving their opportunities to share, the statistics will become even more positive. My experience has been so compelling, that I have a standing guarantee at Applied Focus, a business I direct, that if I cannot improve a business, company or organization, my services are free.

> **Successful leaders empower people.**

Qualities of Leadership

Since this is not a book devoted to building leadership, but one written to help leaders, I will not go into great detail on leadership, per se. However, as stated at the beginning of this chapter, leaders play a very critical part in the maximization of human potential—which I keep calling the *right* bottom line. Thus, there is a need to touch on some basic qualities that provide leaders with the greatest probability of maximizing this important asset. Most of these qualities and profiles are well known. Unfortunately, we frequently observe they are not used. Thus, I felt it necessary to have a short discussion about qualities of leadership. Let me first note a difference between leaders and managers. They are sometimes confused.

We define *managerial* as organizational and mechanical. Organizations need good managers who will see that processes happen according to the prescription determined. Leadership, on the other hand, determines the prescription, unlocks the power in people and facilitates the development of vision and growth. The key to optimizing the organization's success is optimizing people's success. Good management is needed for effectiveness in climbing the ladder. Leadership is needed to make sure that the ladder is against the right wall.

As previously noted there are many ways to classify leaders. For our purpose as it relates to maximizing workers, I have borrowed profiles from the *Love and Logic* philosophy.[20] Basic to the qualities found in leaders in their relationships to subordinates, are at least three types. Although they may be given different names, they are found in every phase of developing people: helicopter leaders, drill sergeant leaders, and counselor leaders.

Helicopter leaders get their name from hovering over their workers. They are afraid that those wonderful folks who work for them might fail. They make sure they check on everything, and make sure it is done correctly. I know an individual who works for helicopter leadership. He is professionally trained, experienced, and very competent. His response to this mode is to be quietly expanding his abilities toward a different job. Of course, he is not the only one in this organization in this situation. This individual is concerned that leadership does not want his recommendations for change and/or improvements. He also feels restricted and confined. Deviations, exploration and development that could improve the company and which once were in his mind are no longer there. Unfortunately, leaving is.

In addition to the failure to capitalize on the most important bottom line, there are other drawbacks for the leaders themselves. First, helicopter leaders can never rest. If they did, they fear things would either self-destruct or at the very least, not function at the optimum. I once worked with a helicopter CEO. He worked late every night, worried a lot about everything, and eventually had a heart attack. Of course, that did not stop him. From his hospital bed he still oversaw the operations. When retirement time came, he kept putting the date back farther and farther. Finally the board of directors set a farewell party date, carried it out, and said goodbye. After he left, the enterprise actually became more successful.

Drill sergeant leaders are much like the helicopter CEO in that they must oversee. However, they are more negative, sometimes even abrasive. They do not just hover; they direct. The message they send to subordinates is not just concern, but that there is only one competent individual around and it is not the subordinates. While under helicopter leaders, people become annoyed and tired of the constant checks and double checks, and get to the point where they do not do a good job, since they know mistakes will be found and taken care of anyway. Under the sergeant, problems are worse.

Drill sergeant leadership results in subordinates responding in one of two ways. One group gets weary of being seen as unappreciated, unintelligent, and incompetent. They get tired of being treated as liabilities instead of assets. They gripe under their breath while inside, and loudly proclaim negative thoughts outside. One of their goals is to take their talents elsewhere. Over time, the loss of good people negatively affects the organization. This makes an even more dramatic impact when combined with the second group.

These people become combative and negatively aggressive; they will not leave. No one is going to push them out. Instead of leaving, they become hostile. They organize unions, undercut leadership, do not support the enterprise, file grievances and lawsuits, and generally spread the negative word to would-be recruits. After awhile, these are the people you wish *would* leave. The dollars that have been spent in dealing with the results of drill sergeant leaders is in the billions. Beyond that, the loss in optimal productivity is as devastating.

Drill sergeant leaders can get results. They are not always good results, however. A school district with a board and superintendent operating from sergeant style—we always know best, and there is no discussion—were dealing with numerous grievances and lawsuits, had a staff that would not support their own district's levy elections, and was spending many dollars in hired negotiators. With leadership change, the district turned around in a year's time. Lawsuits, grievances, and contention vanished. Staff worked with leadership to pass levies, develop programs, and focus on kids.

Our third style—counselor leadership—is based on the McGreggor X-Y theory that assumes human beings are intelligent, want to succeed, and work best alongside people who see them as competent. The counselor leader sees the development of the individual as his/her greatest challenge and most productive asset. Counselor leaders follow the idea that when you give a person a fish, they can eat for a day, but if you teach them *how* to fish, they can produce forever. They also have other qualities. We will spend some more time on them later. First, take a moment and look at you and your group. I know we said we were not all that interested in leadership styles. However, because of the simplicity and the dramatic affect of each of the three, it warrants some study.

Change Activity 12

To get an idea of your leadership style and that of other leaders in the organization, complete the form below. Because many people are not solid in any corner, check the area that fits their dominant mode of operation. It even works at home. Use of these ideas and this review could be a good experience for you to do with other leaders in your organization.

1. List the leaders in your organization.
2. Determine where they best fit.
3. Examine the possibility and/or benefits, or lack there of, if changes were made.

Name initials	Helicopter	Counselor	Sergeant	Comments, Observations, Directions, Benefits of changes
You				

So, what do you do with the information? Always remember that people do whatever they do for a reason. It can be that they were taught or worked in organizations that functioned that way. It could be that it has just been a mode that has, in their eyes, been successful. Regardless of how they, or you, got there, self-acknowledgment is the first key. Second is to decide that some modification to your approach will make a positive difference in the people in the organization and you. Third is to determine in specific situations what a different approach would look like. Fourth, decide what specific changes in specific situations you will make. Until you determine specifically what and how you will modify what you do, the exercise is just that—an exercise.

Application

Carry out number four above. For example, there is an individual who you do not trust to get the job done right. Your usual response is one of the hovering or ordering kind. Not only does that take your time, it does not allow her/him to grow and become more competent. Obviously, if this individual were more independently successful it would give you more time. So, your assignment (which I hope you will accept) is to make sure you:(1) are very clear with any instructions or descriptions; (2) get away from the situation so that you will not be tempted to step in or oversee; (3) be available to help (if you have been a real over-controller, this person may feel abandoned the first time you do this); (4) if called on to help, do it by asking questions that put the necessity for problem solving back on this individual's shoulders as much as possible. Remember that your real intent here is not just to get you off their backs, but to help them develop into strong, aggressive and independent workers who are not afraid to make decisions and solve their own problems. (And of course, should you be captured or fail, we will deny all associations with you…this tape will self-destruct in 5 seconds.)

> **Remember that people always do what they do for a reason.**

In dealing with others in your organization, there are usually a number of approaches. Always be specific in what you expect and how that looks. Merely saying, "You hover over competent people too much," will likely only cause frustration. After all, you are the leader to build your people, so put it in a positive mode: "I notice that you are very conscientious and are concerned about the quality of the work in your department." Then share your objective—which should be well-known by all—that everyone grows and develops, and succeeds, that people are the important part of the operation and that we view them as competent. Thus, you want to work with him/her to help that happen with everyone in his/her area. For example, have the supervisor (Ted) pick an individual that he has been advising (hovering over). Ted will let that worker(Ann) know there is confidence in what she does and how she does it. Ted lets her know that he will refrain from bothering her. Of course, if she has questions or concerns, he is always ready to help. Even better, is for you to explain to Ted what you see in him, and note that you realize he is a bright guy and can come up with a lot of ways to serve and develop those he supervises. Always leave the door open with something like: "If you need suggestions, let me know; maybe I can come up with some ideas."

Lastly, review with Ted. In a couple of weeks, spend some time with him and ask how progress is going. Then offer to come in, in a week or two, to provide another set of eyes to see if you might have other suggestions.

Your effectiveness in this situation will be in proportion to how willing you are to allow others to make recommendations about and to you, and how you approach them.

Humility

That brings up a word that has been maligned for such a long time that I almost hesitate to use it here for fear it will be misinterpreted. That word is *humility*. Before you turn away, hesitate for one moment. What was one of the qualities that came through so strongly and made a short speech echo forever on the battlefield at Gettysburg? It was not a bombastic declaration. It was not threaded through with superiority. It was not a proclamation of greatness. It was not a slap from one side at the other. It was a message of sincerity from the depth of humanness. It was a great example of the true strength of humility.

Humility is a unique and paradoxical quality. If you proclaim you have it, you probably do not. The speech at Gettysburg was also not a moaning about how bad, inept or weak anyone was. Instead, it was a few words presented with a humble, quiet strength declaring that we were indebted to common individuals, that we could learn from their example, and because of what we learned, we would dedicate ourselves to greater effort. And it still brings a chill to the listener with a resolve to be better.

Humility is too often thought of as weakness. Yet the first definition found in most dictionaries does not include the idea of weakness. They do refer to: "not arrogant." It is commonly known and felt that no one likes to work for an arrogant individual. Humility is not being arrogant. I would carry this word further.

In our definition, humility connotes an approachable person—one who is willing to listen. One who is intelligent enough to know that he or she does not know all, does not have all of the answers. A humble person is one who values others, be they CEOs or custodians. Humility is a sign of strength—he or she is not threatened by the opinions of others. A humble individual is self-assured and confident without being haughty and self-centered.

Perhaps as important, a humble person is one who is willing to learn. Common sense tells us that no individual knows it all, although you have probably met individuals who didn't subscribe to that view. As we have already discussed, anyone who expects to succeed at even maintaining his or her progress, must learn. The recipe for failure includes the refusal to keep learning. Life is a dynamic existence. If we fail to grow, we are not merely stagnant; we are falling behind.

Unfortunately, humility is the one principle that routinely finds the greatest leadership resistance. It is unfortunate because, in my experience, the lack of humility—teachableness without pretense—is the most obvious and continual malady I see in mediocre organizations. It is also one of the most powerful concepts in optimal success. It forms a baseline trait that if internalized, will *always* make leaders better and operations more successful.

John Ruskin preached that the first test of a truly great man was humility. In that reference he made it clear that he did not mean doubt of his own power, but that great men have a feeling that greatness is not in them, but through them.

Integrity

Along with humility is integrity. The dictionary definitions of this word usually are built around a standard of uncompromising adherence to ethical and moral principles. It is a quality frequently noted on job descriptions. It is a standard that everyone agrees should be expected of leaders. The acceptance of the principle is very noticeable. Unfortunately, so are the number of incidents that show a lack of the actual application.

Integrity includes honesty and sincerity. It stands for trust and truthfulness. It means that a spoken commitment is just as binding as a written one. It means that what I say I will do, I will do. And, I will carry it out, even if you aren't around to watch me.

Unfortunately, there are leaders who prosper without integrity. Unfortunately, there are those who believe they cannot prosper if they are totally honest. In the competitive and litigious society, there are those who believe anything is fair, that if the other person does not catch it, it is okay to do, or that changing your story—saying one thing to one person and a different thing to another on the same issue—is okay, and that deception is necessary for success.

Of course, when we stop to listen to our own thinking, you and I do not want to work for an individual we cannot trust. Few folks like, trust, or want to work for an individual who has flawed integrity. A leader who cannot be trusted, holds and acts on grudges, or plays sides, will never truly maximize the potential of his or her people; they will never be willing to risk, to lay their needs and concerns out on the table, to totally trust and dedicate. Frequently associates fear that if they share their concerns and weaknesses, instead of being acknowledged and assisted, they will be considered inept and fired. Sadly, I have seen that happen. Remember that there is a difference between not knowing how to do something and getting everyone involved to find the way that will result in the greatest level of success.

Leadership integrity is not something that costs money. Contrary to some common beliefs, it actually makes money. It does not take much training. It comes to fruition when there is a conscientious effort to respect the value and intelligence of each and every individual.

Although it is hard to quantify the positive results of the presence of integrity, our own experiences, the examples we see, and common sense illustrate that it makes a dramatic impact. These often appear as a greater number of ideas produced, a more comfortable and safe atmosphere where individuals ask for help as needed and contribute freely. It will show up in more productive ideas, more overall production, better relationships, reduction in negotiation time, fewer grievances, more company support, and increased worker retention. It will also be noticed in a positive, but non-quantitative attitude that is felt throughout the organization.

I need to make clear a side issue involving integrity—being sincere. Sincerity is a component of integrity. It means that what I say to be real, is real. This is very important to you as a leader. Specifically, I ask you to learn about your people. I have provided exercises that facilitate this. Although these have been presented as exercises, you have been cautioned to take them seriously; they are not merely exercises. They are the real stuff. If you treat them as things to do to make points with your employees, they will backfire and result in less trust and less support. In fact, there will be people who will be extremely offended. If, however, you take them as opportunities to change the way you operate and to develop a better understanding of those with whom you work, they will be very rewarding and productive to all.

Maintaining confidences is another integrity issue. One that should have a big caution sign attached. As people trust you, they will share. Sometimes this sharing will involve personal things, frustrations, and issues that are not meant to be told to you, but will just spill out. It can be information that may or may not have anything to do with the organization. While some people will be focused on the business issues, others will have a need to just talk, to tell someone what is happening in their lives. As a result, you may hear things that would be better not shared with you. You can try to guide discussions away from touchy subjects. Regardless, they may still happen. You must not betray that trust—not with friends, not with family, not with anyone—unless you have permission to do so. Obviously, this does not hold if some individual confides that he or she intends to commit suicide or blow up the bank. Sometimes people share their employment fears or what they do not like about the person they work with. This can be of help to you in working your organization better, but the fact that John just cannot stand Mary, or that Mary would much rather work with Joan, can stay locked in your head.

Vision and a Plan

The best way to predict the future, is to create it.

—Peter Drucker

Sometimes we get confused. We think and operate as if the present determines the future. If we get into that kind of mindset or downstream thinking, we become subjects to whatever happens. A better concept is that the future dictates the present. That is, if you determine where you *want* to be, you have a greater probability of getting there.

Although planning is very important, sometimes we get the cart before the horse. The development of the plan needs to follow the determination of the vision. The vision was what put men on the moon in the timeframe decreed. It was what determined the beginning of this country. Vision is the reason we now fly rapidly across the sky in airplanes that are so large and heavy that reason would say they could not fly. Vision is the driving force behind all significant advancements.

Planning is the second step. While a plan without vision produces mediocrity, vision without a plan wanders. Good leaders need to use both.

This concept is so familiar to leaders, that we need spend no additional time.

A Coach

When the leader leaves the room after a meeting, what is the countenance of those in the room? What are the thoughts in their heads? What are the statements they make to their comrades when the leadership is not present? The answers to these questions can tell a lot about the leader and the likelihood and degree of the organization's success. That is not to say that a leader is always full of good news and happy thoughts. However, are the looks on their faces determination or disgust? Is the talk of how they can get the organization to a higher level, or how to leave the enterprise?

Have you ever watched a football team come out on the field all fired up? They are ready to not only meet the opposition but defeat them. They play harder. They succeed better. They win more often. I am sure you have read a number of accounts of individuals who accomplished great feats not expected. History is full of them; they appear daily. You have probably felt the surge of power or excitement that assisted you in doing a better job. This excitement comes from empowerment and encouragement. It is *our* team. It is *our* game. It is *our* opportunity. Shared vision can bring great power. One of the jobs of a good coach is to be the catalyst to develop shared vision.

Some organizations believe that having special training sessions, walking on hot coals, climbing mountains together, choosing employees of the month, and doing activities together build this attitude. The results of some pretty exhaustive research a few years back trying to find what motivates workers found little evidence that motivational spending made any difference. While some of these many different kinds of activities may be of value, they will never take the place of the demonstrated everyday feeling in the organization that each individual is important, and that leadership respects, listens to, openly supports, and cheers on each person—the results of some of the activities I have already had you do.

Some well-meaning activities can actually result in negative reactions. For example, one company rented an amusement park for a day. They invited all their employees and their families to have a fun day together at no cost. Since leadership had a reputation for not sincerely acknowledging people's efforts, not listening to suggestions, and not being totally trustworthy, the family party was seen as a way to try and buy support and loyalty. Yet, leadership actually wanted to show appreciation.

As an effective coach, you must truly believe in and enthusiastically support your team, not just in words but in all that you do in front of them and behind their backs.

Wise Choices—The Exponential Quality

Successful leadership is all about making wise choices. This should go without saying. Anytime you find a successful organization, you will find wise choices. On the other side, wherever you find mediocrity and failure, poor choices are often the root. Market saturation, styles, location, cost of production, economic trends, or any number of things, even weather, are the culprit behind a less than optimum situation. However, close examination will show that better and wiser choices would have resulted in different outcomes. Simply look at history. What a different world this would be if yesterday and back through time those making decisions could have seen the long-range outcome of their choices. And it does not stop there.

Imagine for a moment what your organization, your business, your home would be like if everyone made the wisest choices! I am not talking just the CEO. I am not thinking merely leadership or middle management. I am talking line workers, custodians, delivery people, telephone operators, copy makers, on and on. You develop an organization that gives people (the *right* bottom line) the understanding and the power to make wise choices, and you will have the most productive and effective organization.

Courage

The first act of courage then is simply to see things as they are. No excuses, no explanations, no illusions of wishful progress…[21]

—Peter Block

Leadership takes courage. But the courage I speak of is not the courage often depicted. It is not the bold, have no fear, damn the torpedoes, don't look back stuff. It is the courage to accept the most avoided task: to look at one's self, and as Block says, "…see things as they are." It is the courage not only to accept, but to solicit and encourage honest evaluation by subordinates. However, the requirement does not stop with recognition; it is a step, only a step. Once again, at Applied Focus we believe there must be two components to success: recognition and focus, and action or application. Thus, it is not enough just to accept; there must be the courage to apply, to use the information gathered to improve yourself, your leadership, and the organization. It is not easy, nor comfortable. Nothing that takes courage is. If you are really interested in maximizing your effectiveness and the success of the organization, you must have the courage to address this area.

Sometimes it may appear that I am advocating a weakening in leadership and leadership responsibilities. As we already discussed on the issue of humility, that is not true. By empowering others, leaders do not diminish their power nor their responsibility. They do not even reduce their work load—merely change it. It takes a more dedicated, more honest, and more secure and courageous person to move into an empowering leadership role. The catch that must be faced is that when a leader empowers others, he or she does not lesson his or her responsibility. Regardless of who makes the decision, the leader will always be held accountable. It is like the analogy I share with middle managers, "in our world, it is always the leader of the flock who gets shot first." (To that, the clerical staffs would add, "but we have to pick up the feathers.") Leadership takes the courage to accept final responsibility.

Effective leadership takes courage not only to tackle tough problems and deal with uncomfortable situations, but to trust one's self enough to walk to the edge of the light. You must dare to push into the unknown, to take risks, to look into the future and share the vision with others, and to climb the hill and pull others up. It takes far more courage to trust and empower others than to make the decisions alone or stay in one's comfort zone.

This book is dedicated to leaders with courage, who are not afraid to look at themselves, how they operate, and review the entire organization's mode of operation; and critically important, who are willing to change.

Change Activity 13

An important goal of this book is for you to look at yourself and to view your organization as objectively as possible. This takes a certain amount of maturity and sometimes a willingness to accept unpleasant information. However, growth only comes when we are willing to look at reality. In every organization there is information that is easily obtained. The activity below is only an example. You may think of a number of other items that should be included. If you do, add them. Looking back through the year make the following determinations:

1. By month, list the number of individuals who quit the organization.
2. Is the trend positive or negative?
3. By month, list the number of grievances and lawsuits filed against the organization.
4. Is the trend positive or negative?
5. By month, list the number of complaints logged.
6. Is the trend positive or negative?
7. Do you have a means for members to express complaints?
8. Has this been effective?
9. Why or why not?
10. By the month, how many registered positive comments have been logged?
11. Is the trend positive or negative?

After tabulating the information, compare it with previous months and years, review reasons, and make any other analysis that will help you improve the organization.

Month	J	F	M	A	M	J	J	A	S	O	N	D	Total
Number who quit													
Observations:													
Grievances etc.													
Observations:													
Complaints													
Observations:													
Positive Comments													
Observations:													

After reviewing the information from this last activity, you may determine that things are okay or that the cost is insignificant. If that is true, great! However, you should look very carefully at the total operation and organization to ensure that you will continue doing the things that are helpful to people and ultimately the organization. To help you more objectively see the financial impact of personnel problems, I have included Change Activity 14.

Change Activity 14

Personnel Practices: the Cost of Employee Turnover

Sometimes we do not realize the cost of personnel practices. In addition to less than optimal output, ineffective practices result is higher staff turnover and significant costs. Obviously, an increase in cost has the same affect as a decrease in revenue, and reduced costs are as effective as an increase in sales. Thus, a review of employee turnover can be helpful and often profitable. To help you, I have developed this simple form. It does not answer the "why" and "how," but does provide a look at the "what."

To answer the questions below, take the figures requested from your current year to date. To see trends, you may wish to do the same for the previous years, and then compare. I have used "number" as the indicator. If your organization has had a significant change in size, the use of "percentage" in the place of "number" may provide a better frame of reference. If your organization is large with many employees, you may wish to break this examination down by department, plants, etc. for a more accurate picture of personnel practices.

Hiring

1. Number of staff turnover for the time period_____
2. Number of new hires required to re-staff_____
3. On average, the number of hours it take for the personnel department to advertise, screen, interview, and hire a new employee_____
4. The average wage of the persons doing the hiring process $_____
5. Multiply the number of new hires (#2 above) by the number of hours required to hire (#3) by the average wage (#5) and put that number here $_____[cost to re-hire staff]

Training

6. On the average, the number of hours of training required for each new staff member before he/she can assume full duty_____
7. The average wage of the trainers $_____
8. Multiply the number of new hires (#2-above) by the number of hours required to train (#5) by the trainer average wage (#6) and put it here $_____[cost to train new hires]
9. If you pay trainees during non-producing training, add that total cost here $_____

Production

10. On average, the time it takes a new employee to reach the level of proficiency and output expected of current employees_____
11. Estimate the average cost of reduced production difference between a new employee and a current employee during this production-learning period $_____

12. Multiply the average number of new employees (#2) by the length of time to proficiency (#8) by the reduced production cost (#9) and put it here $_____[learning curve costs]

Total Cost

Total cost of hiring a new individual:

Hiring costs (#5)	$_____
Training costs (#8 & #9)	$_____
Production costs (#11)	$_____
Total cost	$_____

Using the Information

The information you gathered from the last activity is *what* has happened. That can be helpful. Discovering *why* it is happening, however, is the greatest value. Depending on the size of your organization, you can do the following by departments, positions, locations, divisions, or by the total organization. The key to success is getting everyone's input.

Start with a simple questionnaire that provides the information from the *Cost of Employee Turnover* and request comments and suggestions regarding each facet: hiring, training, production, and most importantly, their opinions on why people leave the organization. The next step should be group discussions ending with a summary and recommendations. As a followup, leadership should utilize the information and implement alterations. Finally, to provide an evaluation of progress, a periodic review of employee turnover and review with the staff will validate the process and should result in an improvement not only in employee retention but also in staff support and morale.

A word about exit interviews. Many organizations use exit interviews as an effort to obtain various kinds of information. In my experience, exit interviews provide very little meaningful, accurate information. Most of the individuals leaving your organization because of negative experiences will not make them known while those leaving because of changes that have nothing to do with their work, will provide that information. The result will be records that are inaccurate and even misleading. Use exit interviews if you like, but understand their limitations.

The Power of Your Position

Before we leave this chapter, let me remind you of the advantage of the power of your position. At first glance that may seem out of line with the general feeling of this book. Let me clarify. Leadership power is too often seen and perceived as negative. It is seen by many as the power to force or coerce. It is also perceived as permissive—allowing those that have it to operate as they wish—in some cases, even outside the law. Unfortunately, there are far too many examples that support those beliefs. If you are operating with people who have had to deal with leaders who fit those negative images, it will take longer for you to establish a different view. Even then, there will always be those who will not completely trust. However, it is worth the effort.

One of the real advantages that come with the power of your position is that you are seen as a special person. This has nothing to do with your abilities, experience, or what have you. It is the position that makes the power. For example, I have met several governors. Prior to meeting the first one, I was excited and nervous. As time passed, and I got to know other important individuals, I found them normal and even flawed. When I was in the leadership of very small units, I used to be in awe of those in larger ones. However, eventually, I attained leadership roles in organizations many times their size. Now I was more important than they were! Or was I? Always remember, it is not you; it is the *position*.

As a result, a visit from you and a demonstrated genuine concern for staff goes farther because of your position. If you were a regular line worker, for example, and you visited other line workers, it would be an uneventful and mundane event. If you are the head of the company, however, a different response will occur. One example. The superintendent of a significantly large school district was in the community and in an elevator. One of the people that happened to be in that elevator at the same time was a teacher in his district. She recognized him, introduced herself, and told him about a project she was working on with kids. He stated that he would like to see that. Of course, she invited him to her school even though she knew he would never come. A few days later, this teacher was elated to see her superintendent walk into her class. I heard this story from the teacher who happened to be in a graduate course I was teaching. The positive affect this situation had was very apparent. The delight in her eyes and the enthusiasm with which she shared the story illustrated the impact the event had, even though it had happened a couple of years in the past.

Your position has power regardless of who you are or what you have done. Use it to build your staff. Of course, as always, anytime you build someone else, you build you.

Summary

There are many traits that the best leaders possess and exhibit. These are just a few basics that need to be faced and that help clarify leadership's role, particularly in developing the correct bottom line, regardless of the organization, regardless of the size. They are not difficult to understand; they are logical. They are traits with which we are familiar. They are qualities we want to find in those who lead us.

I have worked with a wide spectrum of individuals, some with yearly income that will surpass my lifetime earnings and others, such as pre-school children, who are pleased with a penny. I have listened to people who are considered business or education kings, and to those whose leadership sense could be lapped by a primary school child. The dividing line between them to a significant degree was the understanding and application of these basics. Note that once again I emphasize the application. As I have said already in this book, and I will say again: nodding one's head in agreement is a waste of time; it is what you *do* with what you know that makes the difference.

Sometimes we focus on the demands of leadership because it seems like there are so many; there are. As a result, we do not change *ourselves* much. Translated, that may mean that you really don't want to do the things I am asking you to do. You do not have time for these *exercises*. In my experience, you do not have time *not* to do them. Using the practices and the principles of this book, I have been able to take institutions in turmoil, running in size from a few to hundreds of workers, and transform them into positive and productive organizations. And to do that in a few months, regardless of how long they were in contention. Your choice—stay as you are and things will stay as they are, or as often happens, they will get worse—or begin your work on the right bottom line, and watch things improve.

Change Activity 15

Face leadership reality. You are the leader. That does not mean that you stand in the hall and direct traffic. A good leader is like a boat that has passed—the wake or ripple it created can affect objects even out of sight. Complete the form below. It will help you align what you want with where you are.

1. As I look around, I note the following qualities that I appreciate in others as they work with me.

_____

_____

_____

2. As I look around, I note the following qualities that I would like to see exhibited more often in those who work with me.

_____

_____

_____

3. Measure your own actions and interactions against what you have written. Also, measure them against the qualities we have noted in this section.

Application

The activity above is academic. Some action must be taken. What change could and will you make in you today?

_____

_____

_____

6

DEALING WITH PERCEPTION

The Significance of Perception—As a Man Thinketh

In dealing with perception, two things should be kept in mind. First, perceptions play a very imposing part in our lives. Second, we deal with facts from *our* perception. In our lives, this looks like: she is precise—she is picky; the weather is nice and warm—it is too hot; it is late—the night is young; Ford is the best—Chevrolets are better; chocolate is yummy—chocolate, no thank you; opinions on foods, colors, cars, hair, clothes, schools, perfumes, animals, flowers, hobbies, jobs, movies, television shows, even chewing gum, it matters little the subject, there is no end.

When we stop and think, there are as many opinions about things as there are people to think about them. Many objects and situations are comparatively easy to evaluate, yet we still have differences. What really is the true color of blue? How fast is too fast? What kind of dog is the greatest pet? Which toothpaste is the best? The more abstract the situation or the less experience with it, the more likely there will be differences. And, as noted above, these present themselves in our lives at every corner.

Although different opinions are not necessarily bad, they often cause problems. Frequently, the greatest conflict comes when we do know or, more likely, we *think* we know, what is going on. This "think we know"—our perception—is the critical component. We usually do more than just think our perception; we also act in response. Since it may be totally different from someone else's perception and their choice of action, this is an area fraught with traps. It is an area that ultimately causes many problems.

Perception is Fact

Once upon a time, I debated the topic "perception is fact." The argument from the other side was that whatever is real is real and it does not matter what one perceives. Although I do not totally disagree with that thinking, to me, it does not say enough. Individuals operate based on what they perceive as fact. It then actually becomes the fact. Additionally, there are many things where a completely accurate definition of "fact" is not possible. In those situations what is perceived as fact is fact.

First let us explore the principle as it operates with people in real life. The important cornerstone of this principle is that human beings operate from perception. More precisely, they operate from *their* perception. They can be correct, partially correct, or absolutely in error.

Let us look at an example that argues it does not matter what one perceives, fact is fact. The driver of a car on an icy road may not perceive the ice. Yet if he or she hits an icy spot, needs to stop suddenly or makes a turn too quickly, the physics of the situation still come into play. Obviously, fact has an effect. What gets the driver in trouble, however, is perception and the inability to change that perception quickly enough upon discovering a new fact. The driver drives like the road is not icy. He or she finds out differently when there is a need for a quick stop. At the moment the quick stop is required, the perception changes. The road is icy! Regardless of the impact of the wrong perception, the perception-is-fact idea may result in another kind of impact. Obviously, if the road is too icy for traction, it is too icy for traction. And all of the difference in perception will not change the fact. That is, of course, why there are accidents.

In less physical things, perception may be less exacting. If your employees believe you to be the enemy, many things you do even in a positive way may be perceived negatively. Let me share an example.

There was a school district that had a program designed to help heal personnel wounds and foster appreciation. It was based on the sound reasoning that when you serve individuals and get to know them, you like them better. In practice, it went something like this: everyone in the district was to pick someone he or she did not particularly care for. The assignment then was to do good things for them throughout the year. At the end of the year everyone would take off their masks, so to speak, and share who they were. The usual result was a greater and closer bond—an interesting concept.

As the superintendent told it, because of his position, the size of the district, and the many decisions he had to make, he expected any number of folks to have somewhat negative feelings toward him. At the end of this particular year, however, he was shocked! When he was given the name of the person who had been providing thoughtful gifts to him, he could not believe it. This was a person he knew personally, who he had conversed with on a number of occasions, and who he thought of as a friend. He went to the individual and said, "I had no idea you disliked me. Whatever did I do to you that caused this feeling?"

Her honest reply was extremely enlightening. "Do you remember when you came into our school and the faculty lounge one day? I had provided you with a very good idea. Do you remember what you said?" she asked. The superintendent remembered the event, but could not think of anything that should have upset her, let alone leave a lasting, negative feeling. She answered the question by saying, "You said to me, 'what a great idea, *where did you get it?*'"

The superintendent was paying this teacher a compliment; he was acknowledging her for a great idea. However, she perceived it to be an insult. She heard, "After all stupid, you could never come up with such a great idea. You must have gotten it from someone else!"

Perceptions are real, are colored by what individuals believe, and affect their thinking and actions. Perceptions are also very closely tied to emotions, as noted in the two examples. Too often we ignore, discount or avoid feelings. They are often not predictable, they are time consuming and not easy to deal with, and they can detract from the organization's operation. As Kayser, in *14 Collaborative Principles*, notes: "I've learned that emotions are not something managers, team leaders, or team members are comfortable facilitating. That is understandable. Still, it must be done to preserve teamwork and collaboration. While you are never ask to agree with the emotions being expressed, you must never deny people the feelings they are expressing."[22]

People are emotional creatures. Some consider this a weakness and deny their infection, as it were. The interesting thing about even these non-emotional people is that if you insist strongly enough that they are emotional, their rebuttal will become emotional. Often, the more emotional we become, the more our perception is affected.

> **Successful leaders understand that people are different and capitalize on those differences.**

Change Activity 16

Do a hindsight check. On the form below, note events that have happened in a period of time—one or two weeks—that illustrate perception differences. This can be from work, home, the news, or whatever. Note how a change of perception could affect the situation significantly.

Situation Observed	Other Possible Perceptions or Interpretations	Affect of Those Different Perceptions or Interpretations

Thinking and Learning Styles

There is an understanding long known by educators that has to do with the way kids (and adults) think and learn. According to research, some of that appears to be "hard-wired" in us. That is, we seem to have been born with it. These predispositions influence the way we approach tasks or problems, what aspects of a program on which we focus, and how we learn. Obviously these "learning styles" have a significant affect on how we perceive everything we encounter in life. Have you ever noticed that some people have everything neat and tidy while others seem to let things scatter? Have you noticed how some people always seem to have big ideas or visions but not a lot of detail in their plan? You may know someone who seems obsessed with what you perceive as inconsequential minutia. On the other hand, you may have the opinion that some individuals need to get their feet on the ground and generate details and a succinct process.

If you pay attention, you can see it plainly in a marriage relationship, friendships, organizations, at work, your kids, and even the mother-in-law. Actually, under the right situation and pairing, the differences can be helpful. Once again, however, learning styles affect our perceptions. And, once again, we tend to believe our style—our way of thinking—is the *right* way. Obviously, that means that those who do not think as we do are *wrong*, or if we want to be more positive, not as right. Failure to recognize these traits can be more than an irritant. Even simple things can cause friction, like the way the toilet paper roll should be put on the roller—paper feed over the top or under—nicknacks on the counter or not, food separated on the plate or all together, layout of drawers and closets, etc. And we haven't even thrown in the situations at work.

The first rule is to remember that an operation different from yours is not wrong, stupid, or done as an irritant to you. Having everything in a very ordered way, even in a tight sequence is no more right or wrong than a more random pattern. At that statement, I often get a response from the group of people we call analytic-sequential. They think that without their perception of order little can be accomplished. As the father of a couple of kids who were pretty abstract-random, my typical comment upon entering their rooms was, "This is a mess, I'll bet you can't find anything." Of course, this perceived challenge was often met with an illustration of the fact that they could indeed find whatever I requested.

Different styles do lend themselves to more effectiveness in selected situations. However, as I stated in the preceding paragraph, the perceptions others have are not wrong, stupid, or done as an irritant to you. Realize that these beliefs are felt as part of us. Additionally, when you talk against beliefs, you are likely to get an emotional response that matches the strength with which you present your difference. Be on guard that your reaction to someone else's perception does not send a challenging or negative message.

These learning, thinking and operating styles come from within us for whatever reason, and dictate many of the things we do, and more importantly, how we do them. Although we can and do move outside of our primary thinking and operating style, we prefer our home ground and tend to stay as close to it as our situations allow. And, although it is not the aim of this book to go into this concept in depth—there are a number of good books devoted to the subject—it is important in dealing with people to know that this is real; it does affect perception and ultimately, actions.

Remember that learning and thinking styles are more than academic, they are emotional. Before the next example, again, I want to stress that given a situation, there may be more productive or less productive perceptions. However, how we perceive is not a declaration of "right" or "wrong"—just an acknowledgment that as individuals, we often do see things differently.

Stop! Read Change Activity 17. *Do not* read beyond it until *after* you have completed it.

Change Activity 17

In the blank below do the following:

1.   Read the statement.

2.   Without pondering the question, using the first thoughts that come to mind, write a statement that answers the question.

What do trees have to do with poetry?

I assume you have completed the simple task of *Change Activity 17*. If you have not, go back and do it. If you have completed it, go on.

*   *   *

I was once asked to spend a few minutes with a group of teachers, to help them become acquainted with learning and thinking styles. I asked them to tell me what a tree had to do with poetry. A man in the second row volunteered that trees with their beauty and grandeur inspired poetry. The gentlemen seated directly in front of him, instantly and without thinking, snorted a little laugh. Of course, I called on him. His reply was not meant disrespectfully nor was it given condescendingly—just factually—that plain and simply, trees were wood. Wood was made into paper, and poetry was written on paper! Who was correct? Obviously, they were both correct. After a little discussion, they both could see the other's viewpoint but still did not agree. In each of their eyes, the other perception of "correctness" was not accurate. This knee-jerk reaction illustrated how ingrained these beliefs are. Because not everyone is as strongly aligned as these two individuals, you may not notice as much divergence in styles in the people with whom you work. If you sit back and pay attention, however, you will see the differences.

The point here is not just that there are differences in thinking, but that they are deeply imbedded and can be tied to significant emotional responses. This becomes more impacting when responses tied to the way we think and perceive, are viewed as the way things *really* are. You can imagine if the example used were about a more serious concept, or if these people were working on a project together and did not accept that people think differently naturally, and that it is okay. That dramatic response could not only stand in the way of a successful project but could cause friction that might extend into other events.

Some people are more analytical. They like to pick things apart and look at the pieces. Some of these analytics also are sequential. That is, they not only like things detailed, but they are more comfortable when it is done in a certain manner. They may be completely frustrated by what appears to them to be the less concise function, even chaos, of others.

On the other end of this spectrum are people who see big ideas, but often miss some of the details. They also may be much more comfortable with issues being spread all over the table randomly. These global individuals, especially if they are also random, may view their counterparts as stifled bean counters.

Depending on whose theories of learning style you embrace, there are more classifications of thinking "home bases." I will go no further in this discussion. As already stated, there are a number of books that focus only on this area. A critically important part of this discussion is that people are individuals and are affected by their genetics, environments, and traditions, and also the way they are intellectually wired. This has an impact on their perception and on the way they operate in all facets of their lives, and the way they will most likely continue to work.

A second important point is that thinking styles are not a negative thing. Once you accept the fact that it is okay that people think differently, and after the different players understand and accept this fact and after they decide that each person's view is not right or wrong but is just their view, relations and production smooth out. With a little thought, you can see how putting different thinking styles on the same team can enhance the possibility of a better outcome. These differences and everyone's acceptance of them opens doors to more creative and productive developments.

And, by the way, how did you answer in Activity 17?

Change Activity 18

Let us take a minute and apply what has just been discussed. I am not going into this in depth or complete or complex breakdowns. However, the activity will give you an opportunity to view others perhaps in a different light, and can help you be more effective with people. Go down the list of individuals with whom you deal frequently and see if you can gain a better appreciation for their way of thinking. Measure them against the traits listed below.

1. Analytical: Approaches things from *pieces* first, then puts them together to form the whole. Detail is foremost.

2. Sequential: Is detailed plus must have things ordered; first things first.

3.   Global: Comes in with broad ideas; concept oriented—parts come later.

4.   Abstract: Parts have very loose connections.

Name/Initial	Descriptors observed	Classification summary

The exercise you just completed is not meant to put everyone in a precise box, nor to have you spend hours debating styles. Hopefully, however, it has helped you appreciate some of your fellow workers, or even members of your family. Perhaps you found yourself with a little smile on your face and an "ah, now I see" reaction.

Learning and thinking styles can help or hinder. Since we all have them, it is good for us to recognize our knee-jerk thinking and also where others are coming from. A very useful skill developed in my career has been to first, know from which corner I tend to operate, and second, to learn to bridge over into my less natural side. Thus, although I am a more global and random person, I have learned to be analytical and sequential. The result allows me to better understand and work with others, and to modify the way I operate to better fit the current and specific needs.

Perception can be powerful. There are other things that are important in life and at work and in success. However, the underestimation of the perceptions of people you work with, live with or sell to, can be critical to success. The misperception in American businesses has cost billions of dollars. The understanding of the perception of difference in each facet of the buying market means the difference between sales and surplus stock. The lack of understanding of the perception of leadership and people has caused wars or brought them to their ends.

In the area of our interest here, our objective is to have our workers or employees have a perception—that management is honest and fair; to customers—that the product is worthwhile and worth the cost; to students—that the subject is important; to teachers—that students can learn; to parents—that each child is unique and different, and on and on. Because we operate on our beliefs or perceptions, they have a great impact on whatever we do.

Power of The Three Perceptions

A helpful thing to remember is that there can be at least three perceptions: yours, the other individual's with whom you are dealing, and the actual. Let us take the icy road. You may be cruising along at what you feel is an appropriate and safe driving speed. A policeman may see and stop you because he believes you are going too fast for the road conditions. Both of you may be wrong or right. The only correct critical speed is the one that allows the vehicle to perform as appropriate according to natural laws. That automatically takes into consideration the tires, tread, weight, speed, torque, road surface, and so on. The only way you or the policeman will really know the actual facts would be to make some very complicated measurements.

Continually, the three perceptions come into play in our relationships and interactions with fellow workers, customers, spouses, our children, and others. We draw conclusions from frowns, smiles, words, looks, actions, statements, etc. Be aware and wary as you deal with people. And, while we are looking at others, take a minute to look at you.

Change Activity 19

We have been looking at everyone else. Now let us look at you. One caution. Because of past experiences with the lack of understanding of teachers, workers, family or others, we develop a belief that some of the ways we think or operate are not okay. Often those beliefs affect our actions. In fact, someone may have done this to you, and you may be doing this to someone else, even a child; for example, "Your room is a pig pen; clean up this mess." As you can see, that can be an emotional turn-off. We can learn instead to deal with the concern in a more productive way: "You may feel more comfortable with your room this way, but I want your bed made and clothes picked up anyway." In the following exercise do not let the opinions of others affect your answers; this is not an appraisal of your worth, just where you feel most comfortable. Just for a moment, take a quick look at you. In the ideas below, simply circle the numbers of the items that feel most comfortable to you. *Remember*, there are no right or wrong answers and no one has to see it but you.

1. Items kept in assigned places on shelves.

2. Shoes lined up in my closet

3.   Eating different foods on a plate separately

4.   Brain storming with no restrictions

5.   Wearing certain clothes on certain days of the week

6.   Being spontaneous

7.   Plans presented with details

8.   Using trial and error to problem solve

9.   Finish one task before going on to another

10. Understand the whole idea before going step by step

11. Want to know the rules exactly

12. Read for the overall concept—skip some of the words and ideas

13. Use of imagination

14. Organization

15. Presenting ideas as soon as they come to mind

16. Everyone contribute as they feel need to

17. Flexibility regardless of rank

18. Work with others

19. Practical

20. Patience

21. Routine

22. Completion

23. Assist others

Without using any serious scaling and analysis, it should be easy for you to see where you feel most comfortable. Remember that everyone won't feel the same way, and that is okay. Again, if we are going to be successful working with people—the most important bottom line—we must not only accept that there are differences, but that they are fine, and can be used to advantage. One of the problems as leaders and people that keeps our effectiveness at a lower level is the belief that our idea is the *right* idea, and our answer is *the* answer. And, the flip side, that others' beliefs and ideas are not as good.

Application

Select an individual with whom you often disagree, and that you can identify as a person who just does not think like you do. Before your next meeting with her/him:

1. mentally determine that you will allow him/her to express *totally* her/his opinion,

2. determine that you will make a concerted effort to *really* listen with the reality that this individual's opinion is another way of looking at the issue, and one that others may espouse (really listening means that you will push comebacks, responses, etc. out of your mind and concentrate on what the individual has to say), and

3. determine that you will honestly consider what this person has contributed. I would suggest that you ask questions to make sure you understand this individual's viewpoint. Remembering a previous chapter, can you see some possible positive spin-offs just from your actions of listening to this person?

After you have done this with one person, consider using the process with at least one other person.

<u>Perceptions Can Be Changed</u>

As in the icy road and the superintendent story, perceptions can and do change. Once we understand that someone who thinks differently than we do, or from a different angle, is not necessarily being contrary, our perception of his or her thinking and actions, can change. Likewise, the perceptions of others about you can be changed, too. That is, of course, not automatic. Keep in mind that what is perceived is perceived and you may have to do many things for a long time to bring about a change.

Consistency can make a real difference. Conversely, it does not take many sideways steps to confuse the issue and send the perception back into its original corner. Then too, you may be fighting baggage or past experiences that make it even more difficult. Sometimes we refer to this "baggage" as "tapes." We all carry around with us tapes of conditions and individuals that keep playing in our heads. In fact, the same tapes that keep us from giving the boss another chance because he has been less than fair in the past, keeps us from progressing to a different reaction or perception and making productive changes in our own lives.

Along with consistency, another way to change perception is education or information. I recall a situation that had labor-management problems. The staff did not trust the administration. After assuming the management leadership, I could see why. The staff believed that management had not told them the truth regarding the available funds. The staff was absolutely correct. After I had spent enough time with the staff, they began to believe what I was saying was true, because it was. The union, however, pushed for more than was available, with the attitude that getting the needed funds to pay the increases was management's problem. They did not want to hear the facts. They wanted choices without consequences. Their perception moved from a point of not trusting, to wanting to know, to not wanting to know—just wanting. Their perception was that we could find the money, period. We needed to change that perception.

We did. We invited them to participate in the budget development process, and to help decide where the money would be spent. As they became educated, like it or not, they had to modify their emotional perception and exchange it for a factual one.

Although it may not take us much time to talk about changing perception, the fact is that it usually takes a considerable and consistent effort over a significant amount of time to develop positive perceptions if they were once perceived as negative. But, in a like manner, the gyroscopic procession also plays in the other direction. When we believe things are good, minor and sometimes major problems will not shake the positive aura.

Do not forget the comment, "My mind is made up, don't confuse me with facts." But also remember that perceptions can be changed, though it takes considerable time, education and consistency. And I emphasize *consistency*. Reverting to a former practice after proclaiming a change will set the process back dramatically.

Assumption: Spongy Ground

A caution is in order here. Sometimes, it is said, a little knowledge is a dangerous thing. Sometimes when we think we know what is going on, we really do not. Assumption is a very troublesome thing. Assumption means that we are making a guess. Be careful of guessing. If we are to be effective, we must be careful with what we assume. This is particularly crucial if that assumption will determine decisions or actions. Because perception is real and can play as persuasive a role as actual fact, and because our perception may be as off the wall as the other person's, we can be on very spongy ground. Perhaps an example will help.

The game of gossip is familiar to many. It is usually played by an individual whispering a message into the closest comrade's ear. That individual attempts to pass the information along to the next person. This process is continued until the message has been passed to everyone in the line. The result is frequently a message distorted beyond recognition. This humorous game is not too unlike what often happens in normal communications, only the results are not usually as funny. There are probably at least as many problems caused by misunderstanding as by lack of understanding. When individuals do not know something, they tend to go forward, carefully avoiding the condition. However, when individuals *believe* they understand, they tend to move forward unaware. To add to the problem, they often base subsequent decisions on this inaccurate foundation. These actions may be observed by others, who in turn make assumptions. On and on this procession can go.

After every war or major conflict there are a number of casualties and many injuries of civilian adults and children. These are the result of walking on, picking up, or in some way activating an unexploded device. The results are too often tragic. In the area of perception, be aware and understand the potential for problems caused by assumptions and operating as if everyone knows what you know and operates as you do. Often, there are little bombs just under the surface; step carefully.

Change Activity 20

In the box below, write down a situation where misunderstanding created a problem that perhaps could have been avoided had there been a common perception.

Change Activity 21

In the previous box you identified a problem created by misaligned perception. It is important to identify, but alone is not enough to make a significant difference. If you haven't done it, do it. If you are just reading this book, you are wasting your time—you have to *do* something. You know the saying that if you keep doing what you are doing, you will keep getting what you got. Using the problem above, complete the form below.

Situation	Root perception difference	Change you would make	Estimated time to make a difference	Estimated cost to implement	Estimated money saved or gained, and atmosphere improvement

Change Activity 22

In the previous box, you have worked with an example. Now carry this the next step and to a more productive state. Pick a situation within your organization and analyze it as you did the example. If you cannot think of one, talk with people in the group. They should have several.

Application

This is where the rubber really hits the road.

1.   Determine actual changes to be made.
2.   Determine a timetable to make the changes you have identified.
3.   Set an evaluation date—a time when you will review progress and/or achievement of targeted goal.

<u>The Power of Perception—Thinking Outside the Box</u>

Perhaps by now you believe we have pushed enough on *perception*. Because this is such a powerful concept and plays such an impacting role in the hundreds of situations and the many organizations we have viewed, I would like to take it just a bit further.

In the past, we have heard a lot about thinking "outside the box." The idea here is that we need to look at things from different perceptions; even those that seem foreign to us. A few years back, this was referred to as getting outside your paradigm. Let me give two more examples.

First, let us examine an example of a company and a union. The union insisted that the company should pay higher wages. The company said they were paying all they could and still stay in business. The union workers voted to strike. They did, and stayed out for months. The business closed. After months of subsisting on reduced union funds and credit, the workers were unemployed. Their perceptions had been wrong. Their views and opinions kept them inside the box and outside on the street.

A better ending, and one of thinking outside the box involves a true story about a golfer in a tournament. After hitting the ball onto the green, he found it had made a hole in one…so to speak. The *hole* was a paper bag that had blown from a careless observer, and had ended up in just the right place for the golf ball to roll into. The golfer was caught in a very difficult spot. If he took the ball from the sack, it would be counted a stroke. If he hit the ball while it was inside the bag, it was very unlikely that it would move with the accuracy needed. What to do? Using his power to view things in many different ways, he ingeniously lit fire to the sack. The result left the ball sitting in full view with little to obstruct his shot. It was his ability to perceive things from different attitudes that provided the ability to make the best decision.

The lack of understanding how others think, and/or disregarding their thinking causes billions of dollars in lost business, jobs, and waste of human potential. It also causes considerable pain and unhappiness in relationships. One of your challenges as a leader is to walk around perceptions and look at them from as many sides as you possibly can.

Application

This application is very much like the one you did with learning styles, only with a little different slant. The difference is that learning and operating styles are pretty solidly based in our way of thinking, while perception may change with each encounter. Both require you as a leader to be very ready to learn and listen. This application also provides a more concrete structure.
Examine your perceptions.

1.   By the end of this week, pick someone with which you have a difference.

2.   Require yourself to examine the difference from as many directions as possible—as if you were an outsider.

3.   Talk with the person with an honest and sincere desire to learn more about his or her view of the interest or issue. *Do not* spend your time rebutting these differences in you mind while you are listening or verbally after listening. The objective is not to win the argument, change the situation, or fix anything. It is merely an exercise for you to practice seeing as others see. It will be invaluable if you make yourself do it. Actually try to think from that individual's perspective.

4.   On the form below, write down what you have learned.

Name/Initial	What I learned	How this could prove helpful to me

7

THE MOST EXPANDABLE ASSETS

…all of this highfalutin "stuff" about running companies boils down—surprise!—to the folks who actually do the work: ad copywriters, movie cameramen, nurses, technicians, teachers, and hotel housekeepers. "People," "they," "them" always were important; they always were "our important asset," as so many annual reports mindlessly proclaim. But now "they" really *are* important.[23]

—Tom Peters

> The most important asset you have in your organization is people.

In a world of computers and robotics, the hard-wired, complex, quick to complain, hard to understand, hunk of blood and cells component—that human being in the chair over there—is your ticket to success or failure. People are the productive bottom line. Of course, this is not a new revelation. It is one, however, that many leaders believe they have in hand. Careful review suggests that they generally need to look more closely. While everything may appear to be going well, as I view groups with as few as two and as many as thousands of members in professional offices, retail stores, manufacturing, wholesale, education, and wherever people work, I find more often than not, that it is not the case. This should be a cause for concern if your desire is to truly have optimal results. Because many leaders do not see this problem, it becomes even more dangerous. This, however, tends to be a pattern too often present in this country—we believe there are no fires until we are standing in the ashes.

> *Stating* that the most important asset you have in your organization is people makes little difference unless your operation demonstrates that belief; if others can't see it and/or if your people do not feel it, it is not there.

People

People—it is a simple word. However, it represents the most important component in the universe. Stephen Covey (*The 7-Habits of Highly Effective People*)[24] believes that everything starts with people, and that they should be considered the highest value because they produce everything. Often our talk is like that but, as noted above, our walk is not. In our businesses, our organizations, our schools, and even our homes, too often how we operate is incongruent with what we say.

Of all the organisms and objects on this planet, people hold the keys to our success and our happiness. It is important for their good, our good, and the organization's good that we address this subject with profound thought. Ironically, it sometimes appears that we treat our animals more carefully. Unlike dealing with horses, dogs, or cats with which we have very little in common, we really ought to have more ability and a greater desire to positively deal with human beings, our own species, than with any other entity. We say and believe we do, but do we?

This whole topic may sound completely absurd, perhaps even offensive. In my observations of organization after organization and my interviews with hundreds of workers, as I stated earlier, people do not feel as if they are being treated as they should be treated. They do not feel respected as they feel they should be respected. Policies, procedures, and most often, practices do not appear to value people as the priority. Although created by people, they seem to lack the recognition of how people think, feel and act. Thus, let us start there.

A word of caution: as I review these areas, you may find yourself strongly disagreeing. On the other hand, you may be agreeing totally and wondering why other organizations' leaders do not seem to get the word. Both of these views can be stifling. From my experience and observations, those attitudes are the core of the problem; look objectively at your own operation.

You are human. If you look inside yourself or observe your own thoughts, feelings and actions, you will better understand how others feel, think, and perform. That is a key. You want others to respect your thinking, to show appreciation, to treat you fairly, to care about you, and so on. Of course, there are differences, and we will talk about some of those. Basically, however, you can learn much about working with others by observing yourself. What bothers you about the people you work for? What would make your part in the organization more enjoyable? What is your biggest gripe? Start off by doing the next activity.

Change Activity 23

1. In the spaces below list traits and/or habits that **you like** in others. So that you do not end up with a bunch of generalities that sound like the Scout Oath (helpful, courteous, kind, brave, etc.) attach initials of an individual who illustrates that trait.

2. Do not put anything in the "comparison" blank.

Traits and/or habits I **like** in those with whom I work	comparison

Change Activity 24

1.   In the spaces below list traits and/or habits that **you do not** like in others.

2.   Do not put anything in the "comparison" blank.

Traits and/or habits I **do not** like in those with whom I work	comparison

Change Activity 25—Reflection

1.   Go back to Activity 23 & 24.

2.   In the column on the right place a "+" sign next to all of those items with which you feel you may have similar traits. A caution: some of us do not want to see negative traits or habits in ourselves, so we lean toward the positive side. Others tend to put themselves down so they rate themselves lower. Neither are helpful. If we are really going to build our strengths and improve on our weaknesses, we need to see ourselves as accurately as possible. No one needs to see this except you. Be as honest as possible. Of course, you will not be totally accurate—if there is such a thing—in your self-appraisal.

After all, no matter how you try, you can only see from your view; everyone has different views to some extent. Just do it. It should start you thinking and will help in the next exercise.

> How we treat people usually has considerable affect on their effectiveness. How we perceive them has a significant impact on how we treat them.

Get To Know Your People

As I have already stated, attention is a critical component to learning about anything, and as many writers have noted, learning is one of the qualities that makes the difference in leaders. Let me add to that statement by saying that it is not just paying attention that matters, but also *what* we pay attention to. Logically, we want to place the highest percentage of focus on the most critical component. The story about the donut and the traffic accident was a good illustration of paying too much attention to the wrong thing and not enough to the important one. I might add that not paying attention to your greatest asset may not create a wreck, but it certainly may result in problems and prevent you from reaching a major goal of this book—optimal success.

Let me stop here for just a moment. My biggest concern is that what you will read throughout the next few pages will seem so basic and so trite that you will not pay attention, won't do the activities, might even discard this book and go back to your Senge, Covey, Wall Street Journal, et al. First, I would encourage you to read other books—no question. But not at the expense of neglecting this. What will be discussed and what seems so basic, is the crux of what I see the lack of almost everywhere, and what I hear people universally complaining about. Thus, I am being as plain and straightforward as I can be; the problem begs to be fixed. Like the flat tire we already talked about, painting it black, pumping air into it, making it shiny, making sure it has good tread, or whatever, will not make it useful if it remains flat. Or, to use Tom Peters: "*…all of this highfalutin 'stuff' about running companies boils down…to—surprise! people…*"[25] The focus has to be on the basics of really understanding and paying attention not to groups or departments, but to individuals. They are the real links that make up the chain. Stay with me.

If you believe as I do that people are the most important cog in any set of wheels, then you must get to know them. Not only will that serve you in regular everyday relationships, it will be even more productive in critical times. Airline pilots spend hours studying problems—things that could go wrong—with their aircraft. On top of that they spend more time in simulators experiencing those problems and practicing solutions. Knowing how to take off, cruise, land and handle the airways during normal, good weather operations works okay until things get tight. From that point on, they need to have a much more refined understanding. The better they understand, the more likely they will be successful at meeting challenges.

In dealing with people, unlike pilots working with airplanes, you have a better reference from which to start. After all, you are one of them. Yet as we previously noted, unlike the mechanical consistency of machinery, individuals are not always as predictable; there are differences in people. First, a couple of obvious components that have been discussed, written about, and advised ad infinitum. Strange as it might be, unfortunately, they are still disregarded continually.

> People work the hardest when and because they feel a sense of worth.

How We Know Who We Are

As a teacher, I noted that it was obvious that children operate from how they see themselves. In fact, they and you and me use the reflections of how we see we are treated by others as a strong determination of who we are. There was a saying that I used to use in working with teachers. It went something like this: I am not what I think I am. I am not what you think I am. I am what I think you think I am. If everyone covered their faces or threw up every time you came into the room, you would probably think there was something wrong with you. On the other hand, if they always cheered or clapped, your self-image would be different. Although some people carry with them a set of beliefs that help them fend off aberrant images reflected by others, the smiles, frowns, and responses of others have an impact on how we perceive ourselves. Some specifics should help.

Names

This is one of those things you know. Stay with me. It has been stated over and over, you and I feel it, and it ought to go without saying—never forget the importance of an individual's name. It does not matter whether we like our name or not. When someone calls us by name, we feel a sense of importance not present when they do not. A "hey you…uh…. uh…what's your name" does not tend to inspire a feeling of importance. Remembering names is a challenge. Some simple and well-known approaches can help. We have a better chance of remembering if we will just repeat the name in our mind as soon as we are introduced. Carry a "cheat" sheet—a roster of the people or department you are going to visit. Pick out a few names to remember. Hook them to some personality or visual cue. Learn names and use them. If you are *perfect* at this, skip Activity 26.

Change Activity 26

Yes, *really* do this.

Sure, I know you have heard and tried this before. "Try" is a nice word, but it is a weasel word that really should not be acceptable (you can "weasel" out—accept an effort as good enough). However, your objective is not to make an effort; it is to actually *change* your practices, habits and even thinking to be more productive and satisfying. So, unless you know the names of everyone with whom you work or associate, do the following:

1. Pick someone whose name you really do not know, or you have a problem remembering.

2. Make sure you have the name and the person correct. (It is not very helpful to learn the wrong name. Nor is it appreciated a whole lot either.)

3. Learn the name and connect it to the person. If you wish, and it works for you, use some kind of gimmick, example: the name Grace—identify it with the person being graceful, or completely not— whatever.

4. Use the name with the person several times within the next seven days.

5. Pick a day and record here the number of times you used the name_____

Application

Hopefully you did well in the name exercise. Hopefully you have decided to do that with other individuals, perhaps, even in other settings. However, our objective in this was not to award you the "remembering names" medal. It was to (1) get you in a habit that will help you be more successful, (2) show you the affect it has on others, and (3) start improving the atmosphere and increase the potential in your organization. So, for this activity, review any changes that you have seen in those with whom you have increased the use of their names. What have you noticed? If you have noticed little change, there are reasons. (Remember, we said that all people do what they do for reasons.) If you saw little change it could be from a number of factors. It could be that you used the exercise on individuals who already feel valued. It could be that you have shown your recognition of these individuals in many different ways. It could also be that they don't trust you and are wondering what you are up to. Consistency is the key to all of this. You must continue positive practices until they become you. Even if they saw a positive change, if you stop—don't remember or use the names—the lasting result may be negative; they will wonder why you were so nice for a while and then changed back.

Attention

Yes, I already talked about paying attention. To that general term, I would like to add: pay attention to *individual* people. Actually, part of the name recognition power is tied into a chain: because you remembered my name—paid attention to *me*—I must be important.

Like everything, there is another side to this coin, a downside—insincere attention. Because it is so critical, I will state and restate throughout this book that although these exercises and topics may sound like games—even silly games—they are not. They are simple ways to deal with serious topics, and move you to the most effective mode. Climbing a mountain, we do not stand at the base, and then through some magic or fancy formula, suddenly find ourselves at the top. Successful ascents contain some very simple and practical principles and procedures—like one step after another.

I attended a seminar. One of the areas covered had to do with communication. One of the important aspects being explained was that what we do is more important in communications than what we say. One half of the group—group A—was asked to take a break outside for a few minutes. While these folks were gone, the other half—group B—stayed inside and were instructed on an exercise they were to do during the next session. When the outside people returned, the session continued. The people in the groups were paired—one person from group A with one person from group B. They were to take about three minutes each and tell the other person about themselves. The insiders—group B—had been instructed to look at their watches periodically or stare into space while their companion was sharing. The reaction was obvious. Most sharers were very much aware that the person to whom they were speaking was not giving his or her undivided attention. In fact, a number of them became irritated. Since these people had been sitting next to each other before the exercise, one would think that this would have little affect. It was amazing how much it did have. Even after the explanation by the facilitator that it was merely an exercise, some people were not as trusting and warm to their comrades as before.

While sincerity can be a very powerful positive force, insincerity can be even more impacting—only negatively. I continually advise that as important as it to listen to your people, this process is better left alone if you cannot be sincere. As I said, if you are a jerk and have no intention of changing, be a jerk. People will at least have a reference point from which to work. My recommendation, however, is that if you cannot be sincere, you need to spend considerable energy determining why.

Time

Time is one of the ways we show importance. When we sit down and listen to people, one of the conscious or unconscious impressions they feel is how important they are. This actually affects their view of themselves and, ultimately, what they accomplish. There have been many studies done on this aspect. Let me cite one. The objective of this study was not to determine the importance of spending time with individuals. It was actually to see how our perception of others affects our treatment of them. But it also has other things to tell us.

A group of students was randomly broken into three sub-groups. They were then classified as bright, average, and below average. In this study, the students were not aware of this classification, but the teachers were. However, the teachers were not aware that the students assigned were randomly chosen. They thought that the information about the groups was correct. The observers noted some very interesting happenings and results. For example, the teachers unconsciously gave more time, called wait time—the time they waited for the answer before moving on—for verbal responses to the perceived bright students than to those labeled as slower students. The observation was that hesitation by the "bright" students was because they were assumed to be contemplating the question and coming up with the most profound answer. The "slower" students, on the other hand, were perceived as not knowing the answers. Thus, the teachers saved them the embarrassment of long pauses and anticipated wrong answers by moving quickly on. That says much to us as leaders. An important point here is that the students perceived as bright, performed as bright students. Their outcomes were actually better than the other groups.

Because there are usually other variables in any study, and there were some here, we may not want to jump to a lot of conclusions. A point I would like to make, however, is that people feel more important when we give them time and perceive them as important. You do and I do. You may verify this through your own experiences and feelings.

Change Activity 27

You will use time to improve others.

1. Pick an individual who appears to not view him/herself as very important.

2. Visit with the person. During the visit, ask an opinion question. Make it a *real* question: How do you think we could improve communications? What things could we do that would make individuals feel better about their jobs? What could I do to do a better job?

3. Make sure to give the individual "wait" time to come up with an answer. If after a couple of minutes, the person seems to be at a standstill, say something like, "Look, I know I dropped in unannounced and you haven't had time to consider all the possibilities in your head. So, I'll leave you. You are busy and probably have a lot of things to do; I'll just drop by some other time."

4. Make sure you follow up by coming back and asking the question again. In either case—instant idea, or come back later—take seriously the response. In fact, do some reflective listening, play back what you are told by the person. ("Let me see, if I understand you right, you think we should….")

5. Note any change in the way this person acts, looks, etc. around you.

6. If you can, use an idea or solution presented by this person, and give him/her the credit.

7. If you cannot use the idea or solution, or some adaptation, be able to present an appropriate response to at least one of the recommendations: "I looked at your idea to see how we could make it happen. However, we are going to have to make some other changes that would allow us to implement yours. And, on your suggestion of my shortening meetings, what did you think of the last one?" Be sure you are not just putting out hot air. Every idea won't work. If you have one of those: "you should shoot the supervisor," just be honest. "Sorry, we can't do that." That doesn't mean you can't get some suggestions. We could carry this on and on; you get the idea.

Date	Individual	Description of situation	Description of response

Higher = More Impact

As we have already discussed to some extent, the higher up in the organization you are, the more bang you get for your buck. That is, in relationships with staff or others, because of your leadership position you can have more impact. A caution here. If you are a power-trip person, do not let this carry you away. Do not forget one of the great attributes of leadership is humility; also the related concept that if they aren't following you aren't leading. Remember how you feel about the too frequently seen inappropriate use of position or power. Power, it seems, tends to tempt humans to believe they are something beyond the common folk. That kind of thinking is destructive not only to the organization, but to the individual. Frankly, it is not you anyway; it is the position that sets up the impact. Regardless, you can be a greater positive presences. As a CEO, middle manager, superintendent, or leader of any kind, you can actually use the power or aura of your position to empower others.

I held what I viewed as a very inconsequential position in one of the larger school districts in a particular state. I knew the superintendent, but never felt like I was really all that important. I had decided to leave my position and move. The superintendent asked when I would be loading the truck. I told him. The day came. Several friends came to help. During this process, and to my surprise, the superintendent showed up! He spent considerable time helping move furniture and boxes. The impact of that experience will long be felt. Such an important person—as I viewed him—came and helped insignificant *me*! Logically, was there any reason he could not help? Was his help any greater than the other people who had donated their time? The answer to both, of course, is "no." But, because he was who he was, I felt greater importance.

Again, a strong caution. As a leader, you are expected to be "better." There is little that is as disappointing as a leader who does not live up to a higher standard. We have seen that too frequently in many walks of life from politics to business. True, our logic says that leaders are merely human beings. That makes you, as a leader, just like everyone else. However, everyday people do not view you quite that way. In accepting the position, you get the whole works—good and bad, positive and negative. Predicated on your position, you have the opportunity, I repeat—the *opportunity*—to move individuals to their optimum, our goal, more rapidly than might be done by a person in a lesser position. If we think of ourselves as facilitators, people growers, even servants, our attitude will shape our behavior and dramatically impact the people for whom we provide leadership. Of course, that impact will affect the results of the operation.

Change Activity 28

Do it

Yes, it sounds like a good idea, and it might make a difference. No, it is a proven idea, and it *will* make a difference—if you carry through.

1.   Commit to a date. Make it soon. Tomorrow or the next day that you will be with the organization.(This works at home, too.)

2.   Determine what you will do and to whom. It can be as simple as helping with a load of boxes, providing and delivering a donut, or stopping by and telling the individual that you know he/she has a lot to do, big project (whatever is real) and that you have set aside an hour to do whatever to lessen the load (sort some information, make a chart, etc.). You may get a response that the individual knows how busy you are and that you don't need to. Your response must be that you are still going to help.

3.   Do it!

4.   Record the appropriate information in the box below.

A caution: In your offer and assistance, be careful that you do or say nothing that might indicate that you are helping because the other person is inadequate. You are helping in appreciation; it is just nice to be of service to a fellow worker. That, by the way, is a feeling you want to permeate the organization—that this is not a king, queen, jack, and tens group, but a situation where everyone is just as important as everyone else, and that different people have different assignments. An example: As a superintendent of schools, one of the facts that I did not share openly was that there was only one group that could really shut down the schools. That group was the bus drivers. You could always find people to do most every other job in an emergency, short-term basis. But, by law, only drivers with a special license that required special training and a number of hours behind the wheel of a school bus, could transport children in school buses. If they were not there, buses did not run. So…who was critically important in the day-to-day operations, the superintendent or the bus drivers?

Date	Person of focus	Activity I will do	Observable immediate affect	Observable affect on subsequent days

Note: again, there may not be significant change in relationships with some people due to previous experiences with you or with other leadership. If that happens, try another individual or two, or repeat the attention. Some individuals may not trust what they see; consistency can convince them that you are sincere. And, be sincere. As already cautioned, these activities should not be viewed by you as *just* activities. They are small and concrete so that: (1) you can try them without a major change, (2) you can experience the results and see that they really make a difference, (3) you will be convinced and grow. Yes, you are right, this is not just about changing them; it is also about changing you.

A second note. If you have others who supervise you—upper management, board of directors, etc.— they may think you are using your time inappropriately, or that you do not have enough to do. You need to convince them that there is little as critical as helping the individuals in the organization reach their optimum capacity. Also, do not overdo this to the point that it looks as if you are avoiding your other duties.

Application

On your calendar or planner pick a day and time each week to give a small assistance to someone with whom you work. It would be best to have the actual day of the week change. During those few minutes do something for someone. Again, it can be a very small thing, even a comment or an offer to help. It can be to someone who you take for granted, a person who you have not helped often, an individual who does not like you. Don't make it a big thing. It is the thought that counts. However, do be ready to follow through. Otherwise it becomes a negative or a show of insincerity—like saying to your spouse, "I would be happy to help with the dishes when you need the help." She/he says, "Great, right now!" And, you say, "Well, I have an important paper to do (ball game to see, errand to run, etc.—you fill in the blank), maybe next time." As usual, if you are not willing to move forward, sad as that is, better not say anything.

Organization or Insulation

How do you normally operate within your organization to actually reach as many of your people as possible? It is critical that we examine our processes carefully. Sometimes in our efforts to make things better, we actually make them worse. The way your group is organized can improve effectiveness, build better communications, create more unity, and generally be the structure that facilitates the growth, development and maximization of people and all aspects. It can also be a barrier. For a more complete view of effective patterns that positively affect people, I recommend books by Tom Peters. Peters provides numerous examples. But be careful. In your desire and effort to really improve and to help people and the organization, look at all aspects. Make sure your actions do not result in an opposite condition like the following example.

There was a CEO who had the best interest of his employees at heart. One of his goals was to increase communication and to make sure that employees and customers were heard. As a result he developed regional representatives. These individuals were to provide much greater and quicker help to everyone in the organization. Because those people could handle a lot of the problems, he reasoned, it would also give him more time to actually get into the individual units, get to know people, and make more of a positive difference. The plan sounded good. It sounded logical. However, in his thinking, he failed to view possible problems with the structure and make sure he did not fall into any traps. Unfortunately, in actual operation, his plan made things worse.

Since he did not have to deal with so many of the problems, and because, like most leadership positions, there was always more to do than time to do it, he actual began spending more time in his office. He spent less time in the field. Communications were worse and misunderstandings became more numerous. Because they saw him less, and because some of the regional people were not always as effective as he had been, the workers believed he cared less about them and what they did. That, plus the additional problems of less accurate communication because it had to pass through the regional management, resulted in an overall affect that was negative. Not only did this not build his people and bring the organization closer, it was a factor that eventually cost his job.

The tragedy is obvious. Here was an individual who really wanted to improve things. But instead of making his operation more effective and personable, he merely added a layer of insulation. While insulation may be helpful in some cases, from a leader-worker aspect, it creates mistrust and allows misunderstandings to grow. This exacerbates the problem of not seeing as others see.

In another situation, the leader wanted to analyze the operation statistically. He wanted to share with the organization more information about their progress and data to assist them in being more productive.

Instead of assigning that to someone else, he did it himself; he found it fascinating. Consequently, he spent less and less time in the units. Similar to the results in the previous paragraph, his staff believed him less concerned about them and what they were doing. He became less effective, and eventually lost his job.

Be aware of the problems that come with attempts to improve organization. One help is to bounce the ideas off others and see what they think.

Validation—View it From Their Shoes

It is pretty common knowledge that we do not understand how people feel unless we have been there. I have talked about perception—how people see from their vantage point. The examples above are illustrations about people perception. I have talked about learning and thinking styles—how different individuals naturally see and approach similar situations. I have advised you to give time to people and truly listen. I have noted how our positions affect perception. Thus, if our success, the people's success, and the organization's success are based on how each individual thinks, it is logical for us to do what we can to understand them.

While we cannot literally get inside other's heads, we can use that idea to make a serious effort to walk in their shoes. We can visit them in their work place. We can ask them what they think. We can listen to their concerns. Almost always, we can assist more by asking questions than by telling people what to do. That is a major key in successfully leading an organization and maximizing the potential of human beings (the bottom line).

Two methods are most effective at getting inside someone else's skin.

First, *ask*. This is more than just listening to what is volunteered. It means that you take an active part in learning. Simple, easy, straightforward, not rocket science. Sometimes we spend a great deal of effort and time trying to solve problems, understand situations and deal with perplexities in complex ways. With all of our fancy technology, theories, and ideas, sometimes we pass up the most effective and obvious. It has been my experience, repeated and repeated, that the quickest and most accurate way to find how someone thinks, is to ask them.

The second way to walk in someone's shoes, is to walk in their shoes. "Ah," you say, "this is hardly revelation!" You also note that it cannot be authentically done. Very true. But instead of thinking of negatives, when was the last time you actually tried it? And how does one manage to do that? Of course, like most things of any value, it is not quite as easy to effectively do, as it is to say. Perhaps I can help.

First, in asking questions, and to have straight and honest answers to those questions, there must be trust. That burden is on your shoulders. We will talk about that in a later chapter. But for now, note that the more trust people have in you and your sincerity, the more honest they will be.

The second idea—in the shoes—let me combine with the first one. As much as possible, spend time with the staff in their work stations. For custodians, go visit them in their work rooms, their offices, their lounges, the places they clean. Tag along. For cooks, find them in the kitchens. For line workers, visit them on the line. Where appropriate, you could even help. As a school superintendent, I always found it very effective to put my own name on the substitute list and actually teach someone's class. It improved my validity as an educator, and created a significant comradery; I was one of them. Talk to your people. Ask them simple questions about their work, their families, whatever. If you have not done this before, expect a pretty surface conversation. They will not be sure what you are up to. After all, what does leadership and management want from them? Why are you in their area? What did they do wrong? What bad news are they about to hear? Frankly, and unfortunately, in my experiences of many years, that kind of thinking has much validity. Leadership has that kind of reputation in too many realms. So do not be offended if everyone looks at you with a bit of jaundice; leadership has earned it. These activities are prescribed specifically to help you take a step.

You have to prove yourself. That means you must be consistent. You must not violate any trust they place in you. You must be primarily and genuinely interested in them and how you can be of service. You must not have as a focus how this will improve the organization. My promise is that it will ultimately bring about organizational changes of a positive magnitude you will not believe. But if you approach the workers from that point, forget it. It will blow up in your face. A boy throwing a rock into a pond has no idea of the amount of water his ripple will affect. Focus on the individuals and the ripples will take care of themselves. Again, consistency and constancy are critical.

Your visits will have an exponential affect. These people will talk to other departments and to other people. The more you visit with people, the more real you become. It is always interesting to hear people's derogative comments about the government, for example, as if it were something out there instead of something they are a part of. It is intriguing to listen to the person who calls in sick so he can go on an activity complain about all the people who are dishonest in society. The point is, it is always easy to place negative attributes on those "out there." Once we get to know individuals, we often change our view. "I know she works with that group, but she certainly is not like them," is often the way we maintain our negative group views, while modifying them to take into account personal acquaintances.

Schedule visits. Make visits. Do not allow them to be put in an optional category. Be there. The more time you spend with them, the more they will honestly share. The more they share, the more you will learn, and the more they will get to know you. Ask questions on how they view what is happening in the organization. Invite their suggestions. Listen.

Do not wait for a mandate from them, the union, or whomever. Take the initiative. One of the ways I have reduced tension and union strength was simply to meet requests before they were made. If you are spending time with your people and put yourself in their shoes, you know their opinions and gripes, and their wants and needs.

An elementary school building was old. It had more than its share of leaks and heating problems. However, one of the staff's biggest gripes was that when it rained or when the snow melted, there was a very large mud puddle in front of the building. That meant that staff had to negotiate it coming from their cars. The more significant problem, however, was that every child who had to be anywhere near it, had to walk through it. Well, that is not totally true. Every child *wanted* to and usually did walk through it. The result was wet clothes and wet kids sitting in classrooms and going home after school. Requests had been made to the maintenance people but this did not seem to be a priority. Spending time with the staff, I realized how significant this was to them. As superintendent is was easy for me to make it a priority for the maintenance and grounds people. The puddle was taken care of promptly. I think the personnel attitude in that building could not have been better had I given them all a raise.

The second way I have found very successful, is to invite the different work groups in to talk on a regular basis. Let me emphasize what I just said—they are to "talk," you are to "listen." This is not another in a series of lectures by you.

The total faction or department is often too large and too busy to all come and meet with you. Ask them to designate an individual from their group. If this is a work situation and cannot be covered another way, hire a substitute for them for a couple of hours. That also sends the message that you believe it to be really important. So that you get to know more individuals and hear their input, a good practice is to have the individuals who come every month bring a visitor. Have the regulars rotate the visitors. The amazing thing that happens is that these people begin to work with and support the organization and you. I recall an individual after about six months of meetings saying to me, "I never believed we could talk with you this way." Note that it took *six months* for her to reach that point.

Everything they say will not be positive and what you would like to hear. However, their willingness to share these things with you is a positive sign. And, if it is being thought or said anyway it is better that you are aware. The truth of their perception is not always easy to take, but in their minds, it is real. Only a foolish leader would want to operate on inaccurate information. Thus, not only does this build support and communication, it provides more accurate perceptions and conditions. I would emphasize the word perception—like the blood on my finger example, perceptions may not equate with facts as we see them. Regardless of accuracy, perceptions produce actions.

Change Activity 29

1. Select a small group of individuals.

2. Have a meeting with them in which you explain you would like to get their opinions on the organization.

3. Ask them three questions:

    (1) What do you like about the way the organization is working?

    (2) What would you like to see changed?

    (3) How would you make those changes?

4. If possible have an administrative assistant write down the information. If you do not have such a person, do it yourself. I have included a form on the next page.

Date	Location	Refreshments

Individuals Invited & unit

Person taking notes_____

1. What they like about the organization.

2. What they would like to see changed.

3. Suggestions on how to make the changes.

Change Activity 30

You have started something that will be very valuable to you, the organization and the people. I emphasize *started*. You need to make these meetings part of your regular monthly schedule. Instead of using the form in the preceding activity, merely go around the table and ask for questions, suggestions, problems, or whatever. Although it is a good time for you to explain and answer questions, be sure that your guests dominate the conversation.

Perhaps all of this still sounds like a lot of effort that seems to have little to do with market share or profit and loss. That is absolutely 180 degrees from the fact. The idea that leaders and executives are the gods and the people below should be thankful for what they have, and if they don't like it, then don't let the door hit them as they leave, is thinking that, at best, maintains mediocrity and, at worst can be decidedly destructive to the total organization. I have found the personal contact with people in the organization—particularly those who feel as if their jobs really are not important—is the *single most powerful* tool for success.

Borrowing from the Italian economist, Vilfredo Pareto and quality management pioneer, Dr. Joseph Juran, Stephen Covey applied the 80/20 Rule to organizational problems noting his belief that eighty percent of the problems in organizations are system problems and twenty percent are people. So why spend so much time on people? Because, as Covey notes, if you fix the twenty percent, they will fix the eighty percent. Focus on people.

<u>No One is Perfect</u>

At this point, we need to stop and regroup. You have been asked to do a lot of bending over, so to speak, to become a human being instead of a figurehead. As you go down that path, there will be situations that cannot be fixed. There will be areas of disagreement. When we step into being human, we become vulnerable. Our mistakes become visible. In many organizations there is a tradition of mistrust and negative feelings about management and leadership. In this situation, workers actually dehumanize their leaders. That works against us.

When we are leaders and make honest mistakes and acknowledge our mistakes, a very significant thing happens. Unless it is a real atrocity, our people actually support us more. When we hide our imperfections, it works against us. Not too long ago a president made some very poor choices, and committed acts that were extremely distasteful to many people. Instead of coming forward and admitting his blunders, he lied and attempted to cover them up. The end results were that negative feelings were compounded, more respect and support were lost, and his right to office was in question. As a wise grandmother used to quote to me, "two wrongs, don't make a right." Do not fake it. Do not make excuses. Do not start the blame game. Accept responsibility, apologize, fix it if possible, and move on. Remember, to err is human, to lie about it is a real waste. You may be the leader of a great organization; you are still human. You are not perfect. Even with the best advice and most positive intent, things can and sometimes will go wrong. Being human is not only okay, it is a virtue.

Change Activity 31

This is much like a couple of activities you have already done. If it matches too closely, skip it. If not, do it.

1. Set up a schedule on you calendar to visit subordinates or departments.
2. Make it minimal at first—one a week.
3. Determine that these visits will be visits and not lectures. You are there to sincerely and honestly get to know your people.
4. Listen—don't lecture.
5. Remember names.
6. As soon as you leave the group, jot down a few notes to help you remember the people and their ideas.
7. Act on their ideas if possible.
8, Report back and let them know the results.
9. Acknowledge them for their help, suggestions and ideas.

8

MAXIMIZING THAT ASSET

In the future, vision, commitment, shared power and responsibility will be the dominant principles for organizations, as they have shifted from management in order to control an enterprise, to leadership in order to bring out the best in people and respond quickly to change.[26]

—John Naisbitt

As a preparation for this section, take a minute and do a little cursory evaluation.

Change Activity 32

On the following chart, check the most applicable column for the people in your organization with whom you work. (Hot keys=interests, motivators, etc.)

Person's name or initials	Always needs assistance	Usually needs assist.	Sometimes needs assist.	Seldom needs assist.	Never needs assist.	Training would help	Train. might help	Train. would not help	Hot keys are:

Introduction

You have just examined your beliefs about the people with whom you work. You may have checked some individuals as needing constant assistance or for whom you believe training would be of little value. My experience has been that everyone wants to be independent and competent, and everyone wants to grow and learn. That does not mean they act like it. It also does not mean that everyone has the capability to do anything. However, just like you, everyone wants to feel successful. The *hot keys* are areas that could be used to help you help them achieve competence. Perhaps you could not think of *hot keys* for some of the people who need them. If you have begun talking with and listening to your people as I have outlined previously, you should be able to discover things that are important to these individuals. If not, use some of the exercises set up for you (31, 30 29).

A word about motivation. We talk as if we can motivate others. We read books and go to seminars on motivating others. You were provided a column in the previous activity that asks for keys to motivate. The fact is that no one can motivate anyone. We can push and coerce people. We can encourage people. We can force people to do some things. But only when they are open to learning and listening, can they be truly motivated. We can touch their interests and create inspirational and/or factual information that can be a catalyst to people when they are open to listening or learning. They, however, choose to be or not to be motivated. As Robert Townsend said, "you can't motivate people. That door is locked from the inside. You *can* create a climate in which most of your people will motivate themselves to help the company reach its objectives."[27] Note that Townsend says you can set a climate that will motivate <u>most</u> people. Although improving the atmosphere—making it more people centered—will make significant improvements, even then there will be some who take a long time to become learners and maximizers. However, do not give up. Summarizing the important point: we can only motivate ourselves; in reality, motivation for you comes from you. Thus, that is where we will start.

In motivation and learning, attitude is a very integral component. I find a significant correlation between our attitudes about learning and how much we learn and change. So, in your efforts to maximize your greatest asset—people—and help them motivate themselves, *your* attitude has a dramatic affect. Are you willing to explore, to try things? There is much to learn. And it is distressing to see how few people are willing to pay attention, to motivate themselves and to gather the wisdom available. Just a reminder that when you have limited your motivation to learn and take steps, you have limited your success. If you refuse to be motivated and to learn, you have effectively put yourself in check-mate. Finally, no one knows everything, but most people know something; pay attention.

> **Getting the best people and improving the ones you have are the most important and most productive things you can do.**

Good Coaches Excite and Empower

Going back to some basic ways people operate borrowed from *Love and Logic* philosophy, there are at least three broad observable classifications. You may call them whatever you want. In the program just mentioned, they are referred to as helicopter, drill sergeant, and counselor.

Helicopter leaders hover over their people, making sure that everything is done the correct way—*their* way. Drill sergeants hover with a heavy, directing hand—my way or the highway. Counselors lead, listen, advise, and assist. In maximizing people, in optimizing potential, it is obvious that two of those will not work. In fact, drill sergeants and helicopters are debilitating. They, in effect, *shrink* people. They curtail growth, which in the ever expanding dynamics of life, does more than freeze progress. They actually create an atmosphere that results in less capable people. Basically, the only valid kind of leadership, using this nomenclature, is the counselor.

At first thought, if you are a no-nonsense, get-things-done manager, this may appear to be ineffective. So let us break and expand the mindset of "counselor." A counselor is not only a person who sits quietly, helping others explore options. A counselor is also a person who assists others in gaining vision, wisdom, and skills, and who encourages, inspires and even excites people to move forward. Writers, statesmen, philosophers, and teachers come to mind. They provide that something that gets us to motivate ourselves. As an example, let us take a group of individuals often referred to as motivators, but rarely thought of as counselors: coaches. Let me preface the next paragraph with the acknowledgment that you probably have met some individual coaches who were abusive and mean. These individuals may bear the title of coach. However, in reality they are insecure dictators; we are not talking about them.

The job of a coach is well defined; that is why we are choosing this example. Whereas in most organizations, the leader, CEO or board can actually step in and *play* the game, as it were, coaches cannot. In fact, should they venture too far into the playing arena, their team is penalized. The rules even allow the officials to banish coaches with a police escort if necessary. If more organizations operated with those rules, a significant growth in workers would result. Ultimately, the total organization would be loaded with people who knew their jobs, made quick and appropriate decisions, believed they and their assignments were important to the total success, knew it was up to them, and moved forward with energy and enthusiasm.

Like many leaders and managers, some coaches may spend a lot of time ordering their players around. Examination of the best, however, reveals methods of providing guidance and building skill and competence. Yes, they may do it in a loud voice and with much movement. They know that their enthusiasm is necessary if their players are to be motivated. That goes for leaders in any organization. You do not have to have a loud voice, but if you are not excited about what you are doing, very likely your fellow workers will not be excited either. If you are not excited and convinced of the objectives of the organization, your people are likely to feel the same way. As we have all seen, there are some coaches who seem to disregard the intelligence and efforts of their performers. I have seen this in many organizations I have observed. Some good people stay and take the abuse. However, in my experience viewing many, many coaches, that is not the way the best coaches operate, nor is it the way to attract the best players. Great coaches train, counsel, excite and empower. Effective leaders train, counsel, excite and empower.

> **If good staff members are leaving and people who have reviewed your operation are not interested in joining, something is wrong.**

Throughout this book I keep encouraging you to look in the mirror, to know yourself. While it is pleasant to see our strengths, it is not very comfortable to come face to face with our weaknesses. Intelligently, we all know we are not optimally competent in everything, that we have areas that result in problems for us and others, and that there are things about ourselves that we would like to see changed. Although this may not be comfortable, we are better knowing who we are and what we do well or not so well, than operating from a platform that is not real. In the long run it saves us considerable pain. And just knowing does not mean that everything must be changed. You have your choice to do something about any or none of these areas. Just remember that all choices (and not doing something is as much a choice as taking action) have their consequences. And, as we have already said, you may make your choices, but you do not have the power to modify the consequences.

Change Activity 33

To get a more clear view of yourself and your part as coach, check the most true boxes below. Of course, the best approach for one facet of a task or project may not be the same for another.

Item	Always	Usually	Sometimes	Not often	Never
I provide a complete picture to those who will be handling the project.					
I provide a detailed description of the project.					
I ask for input prior to final plans.					
I encourage modifications.					
I allow modifications without permission.					
I require periodic reviews.					
I offer assistance.					
I allow failure.					
In less than optimal successes, I require those involved to identify problems.					
In less than optimal successes, I require those involved to develop solutions.					
I openly acknowledge successes at whatever level achieved.					
I openly accept responsibility for my part in less than optimal successes.					

Do Unto Others

Probably one of the most well known phrases is *do unto others as you would have them do unto you* (or something similar). What does that have to do with maximizing your most important asset, people? Everything.

Sometimes we in leadership forget that if the title, the position, the education, and the background were stripped away, we would be back to what we really are, human beings. People. Sometimes it takes the loss of a job, an illness or accident, a death or a tragedy, for us to realize that we are as vulnerable and, regardless of title, as common as the person next to us. I don't mean this in a degrading way. Being a member of the human race is an honor. But, deep down, we are all very similar. Among other things, everyone wants to be appreciated. Everyone wants to be safe. Everyone wants to have food to eat, a comfortable place to live, and supportive people around them.

When working with others, keep in mind the thought, "Were I he/she/them, how would I like to be treated?" Then, use the answer as you work with those individuals. It has been my experience that this one guide alone will not only make things run smoother, but also increase support, production and success of the total enterprise. Note that this does not take any training, only concentration and willingness. The less regard for this principle, the more problems you will have, and the more stressful will be your work.

There was a manager who had the responsibility to oversee about forty workers. He was seemingly always abrasive. One of his traits was always being right. The situation did not matter. Each confrontation ended with the worker being in the wrong. For example, one evening after the manager had gone home, an individual dropped in to set up for a presentation scheduled for the next morning. The division head associated with that presentation happened to still be available. Although it was after normal work hours, the division head greeted the visitor, ushered him to the location for the presentation, and provided the assistance and information needed.

The next morning, as the division head was going down the corridor, the manager burst angrily out of his office and, in the presence of a number of other people, began loudly to accost the division head. The manager's theme was that this whole enterprise was his responsibility, and he, and only he, had the authority to deal with the presenter.

Because this was just one episode in a series of well-known inappropriate incidents that had occurred with a number of staff members, the head basically just shrugged it off. In fact, the staff commitment to this manager was basically nonexistent. Optimal success for anyone or anything—leadership, workers or organization—could never be expected in this situation. There are many good leadership principles that are obviously lacking in this example. We will not go into them at this point. I will just say that few people would want to be treated in that manner; a child could do better. In this instance and many others, a little common sense could have made a decided difference, a little thought beforehand, a little treating others as one would be treated.

Of course, all decisions and communications cannot be pleasant for everyone. Leadership is called on to make determinations that do result in pain. Laying off or firing employees is one of those. But the basic principle still works. We all want others to deal with us honestly and with compassion.

There was a principal of a school who was extremely good at firing employees in a way that left honor, hope and good feelings. I recall following one such event. The teacher was not as successful as this principal felt necessary. The principal worked with the teacher, spending time and providing assistance and suggestions. After all of this, however, he still felt that the teacher was not effective enough to continue. The principal's counsel to the ineffective teacher was not to find another teaching job, but that he would be happier and more successful in some other work. As the obvious end approached, the principal helped the teacher look at other kinds of work. As the final conference closed, the teacher expressed his gratitude for the efforts, help and genuine concern. He sincerely thanked the principal. *Thanked* him for being fired? The very sound of that does not seem to make sense. Obviously, that principal treated the teacher the way the principal would have wanted to be treated. Were the results for the school the same? Yes, they were. An individual who was an ineffective teacher was moved out of the profession and toward something wherein he would be more successful. The advice to be hard on the object and soft on the people works well here.

Put yourself in the other person's shoes. No one likes to be embarrassed. No one wants to be treated as unimportant. No one wants to be viewed as a failure. Frankly, there are only two reasons we can attribute to mistreating others: ignorance or insecurity. If you find yourself forgetting to treat others as you would like to be treated, it is time to review why.

Trust, the Sacred Concept

Trust is critical to every other facet of success. Interestingly, trust is one of the easiest qualities to possess. It takes no skill, no education, and no experience. Yet it is one of the most crucial attributes in successful leadership. It is also one we find a large number of workers in a significantly large number of organizations complain they cannot bestow on their leaders. Trust, much the same as the "if they aren't following you aren't leading" concept, is not something we have, but something that is given to us by others. Thus, it is directly tied to the people we develop. It is the pay that only they have power to give. When trust is present, people will go to extraordinary lengths in support. When it is absent, it is crippling.

Although it is actually an easy quality to possess, it is one that must be watched carefully and cultivated. In my experiences with many businesses, organizations and institutions, trust of leadership is lacking. Sometimes this was by default. Sometimes it was earned. In fact, the number one problem with optimal employee-leadership relationships I have observed was built around trust. The message is simply: if you want optimal success, you must create trust.

Of course, creating trust is difficult, more difficulty than it sounds. However, it can be gained in most situations and relationships. Tied to the acquisition of trust are many things.

First, many subordinates come to the organization with a suspicion that all managers and leaders (bosses) are not to be trusted. That attitude—their perception—can slow down your progress at developing trust. Because you fit into the box titled manager, leader, president, CEO, chairman, administrator, supervisor, or whatever, you have a special brand in the middle of your forehead. It has a blinking sign that says, "Caution, this creature may be dangerous; do not trust!"

Second, history provides reinforcement. It does not take an astute academician to see a continual trail of dishonesty ranging from U.S. presidents on down. While these are not the only people being untrustworthy, they are visible, and since publicity is usually focused most heavily at that level, these people are in the news more frequently. Most of us know of people not in leadership who rationalize their dishonesty, or that of their friends. They write it off as fair, to balance the other ills they believe they have suffered. Thus, it is all right for them to function inappropriately, call in when they are not sick, take company materials, etc. As unfair as you may believe it to be, as a leader, you must play by a higher standard.

Third, many workers have authentic personal experiences of leadership violating trust and taking advantage of subordinates.

With all of that great billing, what is a leader to do? There are at least three important elements in developing trust in co-workers and subordinates. They are not fancy or profound, just common sense logic. Once again, look at yourself. What do you require of others before you give them your trust? I do not know what specifics you discover, but let me offer some.

First, they need to have exhibited a series of actions that illustrate they are trustworthy. Second, there must also be a consistent pattern of continuity in their communication and their actions. Third, they must maintain that pattern.

If you mistreat folks, if you say one thing and do another, if you portray something you are not, forget asking for trust. You get what you pay for and probably deserve what you have. However, if that is not the case, start by being careful.

Be sincere. If, for example, you start a program as suggested, of meeting with subordinates and listening to them, make sure that you are sincere. If this is perceived as a game that helps you manipulate people instead of improving trust, you will have degraded and actually increased mistrust. In this and other actions, as I have expressed several times, if you are not making the movement authentically, you are much smarter not to make it at all. Again, if you are a jerk and like being a jerk, then be a jerk—people accept that. This is not one of those things that they say gets worse before it gets better. This is one of those things that will get worse after it gets worse. There must be that fidelity apparent in your actions. You must prove you are trustworthy.

Second, communicate accurately. Communication is the key to much of your leadership success. Conversely, miscommunication sits at the base of many leadership problems. This is a topic that is discussed in a later chapter. Suffice it to say at this point that if you are seeking trust, be careful what you say that could be misleading. Be on guard. We often slant what we say in the most positive way for particular groups or individuals, but if that information turns out to be in conflict group to group, mistrust is created.

Third, consistency shows others where you stand. Advertisers know well this tack. They keep repeating a theme until it becomes part of our vocabulary and thinking. These themes become slogans that everyone knows. Determine what you stand for. What values do you hold that you can maintain? What principles in the organization do you believe? For example, do you really want to listen to what subordinates say? If so, send that message through your actions and your talk, and consistently keep it going.

Make others aware. Be open with what you believe and the direction you are going. In the example above, state your intention—that you are visiting with people and will continue to visit with people because you really want to know what they have to say, and that you value them.

Stay the course. When things are not going well, when you are hearing what you do not want to hear, and when adversity stands in the way, keep on trucking. It is amazing how much support you will maintain, even in tough times. The people need to know that you really do stay by what you have professed. As they see consistency over a period of time, they have something they can hang onto. When you do that in small things or a few things, their belief and trust in you spreads into all things to which you are connected. Of course, this does not mean you cannot change your mind or go in a different direction. The important key is that you share what you are doing and why.

I cannot over stress this principle. The ability to build trust, in my view, is probably the greatest single key to leadership success. Conversely, it is the major detractor to the development of an optimally functioning, smooth-running organization.

Building on Strengths

Many years ago, I worked with a program that taught interviewing and personnel building techniques. The process used interview information for the subsequent staff-building to be done in follow-up meetings. Basically, the interviewer did a little homework after hiring the successful candidate and noted strengths. He or she would then develop a profile of strengths and would invite the person hired to a meeting where these attributes were noted and the individual was encouraged to elaborate on them. The theory was that when people are recognized for the things they do well, they feel good about their accomplishments. Feeling good about ourselves is all well and good, but the ultimate goal was more.

Researchers discovered that when we are acknowledged for what we do, several actions take place. First, we tend to continue those reinforced traits or operations. Second, we feel an obligation to ourselves and others to not be less than what the interviewer believes. And third, we feel better about ourselves and what we do, so we tend to increase our abilities and improve on our practices. In the process, we also improve on our less effective traits and skills.

My actual experience confirms this principle. Let me share an example. I was a school superintendent/principal in a very small school. I prepared for my meeting with a new teacher I had hired. I invited her in and followed the protocol. I pointed out some questions she had answered, and indicated how impressed I was with her answers. I then asked her to share more about her ideas and experiences as they related to each of those items. It was as if a gate had been opened. She went into detail about many of the things she was doing, how she was doing them, and why. She shared the results and the collateral ideas and strategies that spun off these experiences. At the end of the session, I had learned a lot, and she was elated. As she was leaving my office, she thanked me, and without thinking gave me a hug. Did she work harder? Did she feel positive about me as her leader? Did she continue to grow? You already know the answer. Was this a program process I had learned? Yes. Was I using it to manipulate? No. Did it actually make a change in me and the teacher? Yes.

Common sense, logic, and our own feelings and experience set our understanding here. It is only logical that we feel better when someone is noting our best traits. It does create within us a desire to not do less and to not let down those who have faith in us. You may think that to be overrated. Stop for a moment. Remember one of the statements made at the very first of the book—that if everyone in your organization (the correct bottom line) operated at their maximum potential, there would be significant upward movement of your organization.

This approach is appropriate and significantly more productive than its counterpart of reinforcing negatives. No organization can shy away from things that need to be changed and performances that have to be improved. But, as good coaches know, when team members are up, have a glint in their eyes, and can't wait to take on their opponent, they are more likely to do better than if they think only of their mistakes.

Dr. Douglas Ratelle works with college athletic teams. His approach is to have the players visualize successful experiences, to remember the feeling, and to recreate that feeling. He then has them carry that into their present situation. Interestingly, team members involved in this process improve significantly. We are what we think we are.

Again, obviously, mistakes and problems have to be worked out and changes must be made to reduce future non-productive practices. However, the quality of the changes and the future success is dramatically affected by the attitude and process demonstrated by leadership. In considering the goal of optimal success, as we have previously noted, solving problems only results in the lack of problems, not in the greatest success. It is kind of like an overboard boater: getting to the surface of the water is a necessary problem to solve, but it may be a far cry from being where he needs to be to maintain a quality of life.

> **They [people] don't have to be forced or threatened. If they commit themselves to mutual objectives, they'll drive themselves more effectively than you can drive them.**[28]
>
> —Robert Townsend

Change Activity 34

Okay, let us do a "rubber hits the road" activity.

Although you have done some activities that were much like what we have just discussed, it could be very productive for you to review some files of some of the members of your group. You may want to pick individuals who are newer, or with whom you have had less contact. Simply:

1. Jot down some traits or strengths that were noted in the hiring process—particularly those that may not be quite so apparent in the individual's current assignment. If you do not have a written record that shows positive traits, talk with the interviewer.

2. Invite the individual into your office or a place where you won't be bothered. And, by the way, *don't* be bothered; let the phone ring, or have someone take messages for you outside your office. It demonstrates an individual's importance for you to just let it ring. You merely acknowledge that you hear the ring and state that whatever it is, can wait. You cannot establish a "what you say is important attitude" to the person in your office if you keep answering the phone. We have become a society with telephone ear disease; let it ring.

3. Bring up the strengths you have noted and merely say, "tell me more."

Assume They Can: Expectations=Performance

The managers in this company didn't blame their employees…they didn't merely exhort them to "try harder" or "be friendlier." Instead, the employees were involved in the improvement effort, trusted to make intelligent decisions on behalf of the company and its customers.[29]

—Brian L. Joiner

One of the principles of human development that holds true with children and adults is tied to expectations. People perform as expected. If we expect little of them, we send that message to them through the things we say, the questions we ask, the inflections in our voice, the body language we use, and in many other ways of which we are aware and unaware. Of course, the opposite is also true. That is, when we see them as capable and competent, we also send that message.

When we treat people as if they are capable—capable of making intelligent choices and of doing things for themselves—they gain confidence, experience and skills, and *become* capable. We often refer to this as empowerment.

Were you to review the examples in this book, you could separate those actions that build people from those that do not. This is not only a theme of our thinking, it is a standard business-leadership philosophy. Many years ago, Douglas McGregor produced his famous X/Y theory. More currently, people like Robert Greenleaf (*Servant Leadership*), Warren Bennis and Joan Goldsmith (*Learning to Lead*), Stephen Covey (*The 7 Habits of highly Effective People*), and Peter Senge (*The Fifth Discipline*) see people as being competent and a major key to success, and leaders as people builders. Tom Peters (*In Search of Excellence*) provides numerous examples of successful companies that operate from the assumption that people are capable. And because of that assumption, they allow considerable latitude in decision making. Overall, their positive expectations pay off in total success.

To restate the theme of this book: maximize the bottom line with the most potential, your people, and all other aspects and bottom lines will also maximize.

Application

Application in being positive and having positive expectations is easy to say, but often difficult to manage. There are those individuals who are well-meaning, great people, yet just do not seem to be able to motivate themselves to accomplish at the level, or even near the level, of their capabilities. They acknowledge their failure, know that they can and should do better, but just do not seem to get the job done.

Pick at least two individuals and provide assistance so they can (1) feel that they can accomplish, and (2) actually improve. Although this seems like a difficult task that will take some effort and time on your part, I promise you that if you succeed, you will turn these moles into the most dedicated and productive workers and the most appreciative individuals. Of course, remember that when we lift others up, not only are we developing their muscles, we are developing our own.

At this point you may be concerned and question spending the amount of time and attention required to hopefully turn this less than effective person into a worker bee. Obviously, if you are a parent dealing with a child, the value is apparent. However, if you are a supervisor with an already significant workload, it is a valid concern that must be addressed. There may be some candidates you will just have to inform that they have to figure out how to get their priorities lined up and produce as required or leave. This would be especially appropriate for those who do not seem to fit the job; this can actually be a help to them. However, if you have someone who has obvious potential in your organization and has a desire to be involved and succeed, what I am suggesting below can be well worth the effort and time invested.

First, put the concern on their shoulders: "On average, you come in late three times a week. What is your take on that?"

Second, be part of the solution and not the problem: "You understand that in some businesses this works out okay, but in ours, because of what we do and the requirements of those we serve, we have to be here on time. So, how can we help you be here when you need to be?"

Third, get them to write down a simple plan of attack for this week (or next week if this meeting is on Friday). Let me emphasize *simple*. Sometimes we, in our grandiose plan of things, operate at a very complex and high level. When a person is struggling with what we deem as simple things, they cannot succeed with grand objectives and long-range complexities and commitments.

Fourth, be supportive throughout.

Fifth, plan for an evaluation of the plan with the individual. Make it in the near future. A week works well. Although this is not meant to be negative in any way, you may also realize in this mode, should the individual not improve, there is a point where he/she will actually fire him/herself.

9

EFFECTIVE COMMUNICATIONS

One can lack any of the qualities of an organizer—with one exception—and still be effective and successful. That exception is the art of communication. It does not matter what you know about anything if you cannot communicate to your people. In that event you are not even a failure. You're just not there.[30]

—Saul D. Alinsky, *Rules for Radicals*

We have covered considerable territory so far. Throughout, there has been an assumption that you understand one of the most critical components of leadership—communication. Steven Covey, in *The 7 Habits of Highly Effective People*, states: "Communication is the most important skill in life."[31] I would add, it is the most inescapable fact of life. Let me illustrate.

All you need is one other person. It does not matter who, how old, when or where, as long as you are both conscious. (Well, maybe that isn't even necessary; one of you does need to be conscious.) Now, for the next minute—sixty seconds—do not communicate with the other individual. (If only one of you is unconscious, the communicator has to be that one.)

I will assume that you tried my little exercise. What did you learn? Unless you were unconscious, you discovered that you always communicate. I repeat, you *always* communicate. Even if you are unconscious you are communicating! My experience with this little test is that when people are told not to communicate, they stop talking. Of course, many studies and observations have verified we actually communicate more by our actions, looks, and expressions, than by what we say. Usually, when people are told not to communicate, they actually increase their communications. They smile, look away, show physical signs of being uncomfortable, talk with their eyes, and so on. Shutting them down verbally merely modifies the media they use to communicate.

Let me summarize this point. We communicate continually and far beyond what we think we do. Even if you are dead you communicate something, or many things to those who observe you. Be aware.

This chapter is not designed to provide all of the many theories, ideals and practices of communications. An entire book could be written on this subject; a number have. However, because communication is such a key factor in dealing with and optimizing people and organizations, and because people tend not to realize how much they communicate and how impacting their communication can be, it would be a mistake not to review it. The purpose here is to bring into stronger focus some observations that will help you be more aware and effective in communicating. Effective communication is pivotal to successful leadership. In fact, it is essential.

You may have noted that two words were used: *effective* and *communication*. *Communication* is conveying a thought, feeling, concept or idea between two or more parties. Obviously, that can and is done in many ways, as illustrated in our little exercise above. *Effective* means that we communicate what we *want* communicated. That tends to be a significant challenge. We have all had numerous experiences of attempting to send one message and really sending another, or of believing we knew what someone was trying to communicate and realizing at some later time that we misunderstood. Something as simple as the example of my childhood experience of attempting to show my cousin that I had blood on my finger is a prime example of impacting and almost instantaneous communication. But, in conveying the intended message, it was a total flop.

Because of our ineffective communications, too frequently we make mistakes that cause problems and turmoil, and delay desired results. This unproductive phenomena is apparent in our lives, at work, home and everywhere. It wastes more time, costs more money, and results in more personal pain, than any other single factor. It is a component that has the greatest potential for improvement. So you won't just read this and pass on by, let us take a minute and do a little observation. Remember that these simple exercises are part of the step-by-step change that will result in your improved effectiveness with people. Before you do this, however, let me give you an example.

> **It is not communication that is key, but *effective* communication.**

I was standing in a checkout line. As always, I carefully calculated which one was moving the fastest, got into that one, and found (as you already guessed) that it was the one most likely to remain stagnant until the store closed. Of course, the checker (associate, crew member, whatever) was talking about everything from the best hair dye color to why she threw up when she ate apples. Whether she wanted to or not, she was communicating something. The question: is that what she wanted to communicate, or what she was supposed to be communicating? Next, the supervisor noted our apple-throwing-up checker's line was moving very slowly. She investigated, and decided Miss Share-it-all should be operating in a different mode. In fact, a customer just complained about this line and this checker. When this happened, the supervisor had a choice. She could show her sensitivity to the customer's problem by immediately telling the checker to get moving. Of course, that could be done in a grand manner with a long speech on how important customers are, how much store personnel wanted to meet their needs, the motto of the store, or whatever felt like the appropriate thing at the time, sans the Gettysburg Address. Or, she could just say, "get this line moving!" Or, later, in private, she could commend the checker for wanting to show friendliness to the customer, remind her that customers value speed, and discuss strategies for concentrating more on speed and less on talk.

You be the checker. With each of these scenarios what would be the message conveyed to you? Would you feel more important? Would there be a desire kindled within your bosom to be the best checker in the store? If the supervisor chose to upbraid you in front of the customers, would you be thinking some things that you would like to communicate to the supervisor, though probably would not, but would likely be shared with other workers, family or friends?

In situations like the one noted above, numerous communication components will be involved. The words said, the tone used, the emphasis placed, the tempo delivered, the eye focus, the hand gestures, the stance, and so on and on. Okay, now you try one.

Change Activity 35

In the table below, identify a communication situation that had a flaw and/or created a problem. Also, see if you can determine what went wrong and what could or should have been done that would more likely have brought the desired results. This is a good exercise to use with a group. It helps emphasize the impact of components of communication while dealing with real and appropriate circumstances within your organization. If done using several examples, it will make your people more sensitive to communication nuances. Hopefully, it will also affect the way they operate.

A situation that was negatively affected by a communication problem:	
The intended objective (as you believe it to be)	
The problem created	
The flawed component(s)	
What should or could have been done instead	

Application

I will continually emphasize that our goal is to provide awareness *and* change. Often, unless we focus and refocus by constantly working with a concept, there is little change. And, if there is not change, the information is not worth much. Follow through. As a follow-up extension, make copies of the form above, and have yourself and the others in leadership, or whomever you wish, complete at least one a week.

Once a week or at some designated period, routinely meet together and discuss some of these situations. Cautions: (1) this is not a part of evaluation, (2) be sure to keep personalities out of it.—protect names and people. Your objective is to improve effectiveness and skill, to learn to avoid pitfalls, and to learn from each other—to communicate how and what you want communicated.

Remember that communication is not just sending, it is also *receiving*. It is listening as well as telling and learning as well as teaching. To maximize your growth and effectiveness it is imperative that you fully embrace that concept.

> **Communication is something we do even when we do not wish to.**

We Communicate All of the Time

As illustrated at the beginning of this chapter, communication is an entity from which there is no escape. More prominent than a shadow and harder to detach, it follows us everywhere. As paradoxical as it sounds, even when we do not want to communicate, we do. Often when we are trying the hardest to avoid sending a message, we convey the strongest. It does not matter the setting. It can be a department meeting, a casual lunch, comments on the phone, a gesture that we make, or a look as we pass in the hall. All of these "say" something. Attending a meeting or not attending, being vocal or saying nothing, having a smile on your face or a blank stare, all of these send a message. In fact what we say is often far less important than how we say it and how we look when we say it.

Some of the strongest communication happens without saying a word. For example, women smile at passing men more than they do at passing women. That probably is not astounding news. However, while the common belief is that men are more likely to focus on the details of the opposite sex, watch women. As a rule, women are far more attentive and can give more detailed descriptions of the other women they see, than can men. Also, their countenance tends to be less smiley and more negative toward other women.

A simple facial expression—a smile or a frown—can and does convey a message. I am sure you drew quick conclusions from the example above. They may be different from someone else's. Which brings up the crux of the matter: the important factor is not as much the communication vehicle or aura, but the opinions and conclusions drawn as a result. The frown you give me as we pass in the hall may be because you do not like the way I look, are unhappy with my performance, just got off the phone with an angry customer, were thinking about trouble at home, or even that your lunch upset your stomach. If you have a face like mine—that has a natural frown when relaxed—what others see can even be only a characteristic of your looks.

The problem, of course, is that I, as a receiver of your expression, do not know why you frowned when you passed me. My conclusion is affected by everything from my performance to my imagination. If you are my boss, and if I made a mediocre presentation, lost a sale, or have not been doing as well as I thought I should, your look can have considerable affect on me, my stress level, how I feel about my job, how I treat my family, and so on. Of course, you, as the leader, cannot go around all day, every day looking like Snow White. But, as a leader, it is important that you are aware of the influencing impact of what you say, write and very importantly, even how you look.

On the other side of that coin, while it is helpful not to give misleading visual cues accidentally, it is also a dangerous practice to purposefully skew them. I once knew a young lady who so dramatically changed her countenance to match what she was saying and the group she was directing, that it was not only unbelievable, but downright funny. Most of us are not great actors and because there are so many communication indicators, it is best just to know that there is an affect. Do not become paranoid about your expressions and press a certain *button*, so to speak, every time you encounter another human being.

The best communicators are those who convey what they want conveyed with the most fidelity. That is *effective* communication. The question, then, is not *are* you communicating, but *what*.

> *Effective* communication is essential for leadership success.

Basic Elements

Communication can be broken into at least a couple of types: *direct* and *indirect*. Direct is *what* we say or write. Indirect is *how* we say or write and *where* the environment is in which it is presented. Obviously, there is a different message conveyed when I write "fire" in small letters on the board or in large letters. There will be a different response from the crowd if I use the word "fire" in a casual, quiet conversation, or if I shout it hysterically. It is the same word, "fire" (*what*), but in a different method (*how*) and it conveys a different message. If I yell this same word while standing in the middle of the street in a blinding rainstorm, or while seated in a movie theater, there will likely be different responses. That is the affect of the *where* aspect of communication.

We can also break communication into a least four mediums: written, visual, oral, and tactile. Letters, documents and memos are obviously examples of written communications. Actions, demeanor, and pictures are examples of visual. Examples of oral communication include such things as speaking, singing and noises. Tactile is physical touch.

Direct Communication

Face to face, person to person is direct communication. All facets of an interchange are part of direct communication. All of the senses become part of the encounter. We can see, hear, smell, even touch the other individual. Although there can be disadvantageous to direct communication, there are some definite advantages. In face to face communication, you can see the reaction of your communication. You can adjust. You can ask questions. You can decide not to continue in the same manner or with the same topic.

Direct communication also allows you to convey a greater depth of feeling, sincerity, and emphasis. For situations that are unsure, for those where you want someone else to feel how strongly you feel, and when you want immediate response, direct is more appropriate. Children are excellent direct communicators. Having spent a lot of time working in schools, the hugs, looks and actions vividly display and communicate important feelings. Of course, sometimes these have to be interpreted. The little child who tells his daddy that he hates him does not really mean the words that come out, but is sharing something for which he or she does not have an adequate conveyance. Adults, too, often make confused and confusing statements. This is especially true when they are experiencing strong emotions.

As noted earlier, direct communication also often allows a quick evaluation of your action and/or words. The reaction of your proposal to the group or a returned smile by the person in the hall give you a reflection of your action.

Logically, if you are trying to get accurate information, feelings or reactions to an idea; are willing to discuss and change ideas; or want to be sure your idea, sincerity, and attention are conveyed, direct is the best. On the positive side of *direct*, caring is shown through the eyes, body language, voice inflection, touch, and so on. Of course, strong negative feelings also have greater impact face to face. Additionally, if you are attractive looking and/or a skilled and talented presenter, this too can flavor the encounter and affect the final results. Interestingly, the effect can be positive or negative. For example, I have been involved in interview committees where physical attractiveness made a positive impression on one gender, and a negative one on the other.

While all of these variables have effect, the more time you spend with individuals and groups of your organization, the better they know you and the more consistent you are, the less dramatic will be these different factors. If you act out of character, the tendency will be for your associates to play down or even block out this anomaly since this is not really you in their minds. This is another good reason for the leader visiting with the workers face to face. The mere fact of your presence, regardless of what you say, is important. Bringing the custodians to the same board room where executives meet and treating them the same as you would that group is an impacting direct communication.

While face-to-face direct can be very positive and helpful, if you consider this only an approach to give you gain, it will become a negative influence; you will get into problems. An example:

I left a leadership position that I had held for about three years. Within a very short time, I began receiving calls from middle managers in that organization. They were calling me because they had concerns. I asked them why they were calling me. Their answers were all similar—they did not trust their new leader; they were concerned about repercussions. These were not timid managers. They were people who I could always rely on to share what they saw and thought, and who were instrumental in developing improvements in our operation. What had happened? Examination revealed that the individual elevated to my previous position was not trustworthy. He was a likeable, friendly, outgoing guy, met with staff members, and appeared to be sincerely interested in people as well as work. However, people with strong opinions who expressed themselves to him found themselves reassigned to less than favorable spots, and frequently in positions for which they were not well trained. That made their success more difficult and the probability of termination more likely. This deceptive communication jaundiced all other communication.

A side note here. If this fits you as a leader, and if you do not want middle managers second guessing you or providing what could be, at times, negative comments, let them know up front. Use direct and indirect communications to emphasize what you expect and what you will not accept. The end result will be more effective than the one referred to above.

Change Activity 36

This is a very simple exercise, but is meant to illustrate how real your countenance is in direct communication. This depends on your usual approach and how willing you are to move out of your comfort zone. This week, do one or more of the following:

Action	Reaction
1. Smile at someone who you usually do not smile at.	
2. Start your next meeting by standing at the front of the room and without speaking, quietly smile (or frown).	
3. Dream up your own experiment and try it. Do not do something that would be perceived as significantly negative. It can result in uneasiness and mistrust.	

Application

Use Action item number 2 (after doing it) as a topic for a discussion with staff on communication.

Indirect Communication

Obviously, it is not possible for leadership to visit with everyone face to face. In the consideration of time and efficiency, it is not logical or even possible in some cases to meet with everyone for everything. Nor is it necessary. Sometimes distance and situation require written communications. Moreover, some things need to be in writing; it is the best way to make sure that everyone has the same information. Like any tool, however, care must be used. The following is an amusing illustration I ran across several years ago. I do not know the original source, but I have found several versions. Here is one. It is called "The Story of the Water Closet."

A newly married British couple, looking for a house in the country, found one that they decided was suitable. On their way home, the young wife happened to think they had not noticed a water closet (toilet) in the place, so she decided to write to the real estate man about it.

Being very modest she hesitated about writing the words "water closet," so she referred to it as the W.C. The real estate man interpreted it to mean the Western Church near there, and answered as follows:

Dear Madam:

I regret very much the delay in answering your letter, but I now take the pleasure of informing you that the W.C. is located about nine miles from here and is capable of seating 1,266 people; this is very fortunate indeed.

If you are not in the habit of going regularly, no doubt you will be interested to know that a great many people take their lunch and make a day of it. Others who cannot spare the time usually arrive just in time, but are generally in too big a hurry to wait if the place is crowded.

The first time my wife and I went was six years ago, and we had to stand up all the time.

It might interest you to know they are planning to hold a bazaar in the near future to raise money for plush seats. I might mention that it pains me greatly to not be able to go more frequently. It surely is through no lack of desire, but as we grow older it seems more of an effort, particularly in cold weather.

Obviously, written communications can lead to different conclusions.

Regardless of writing ability, it is more difficult to convey feelings in writing. One of the problems with written communication is that there is no way to explain something that might be misread or misinterpreted by the reader. Visual cues and inflections are absent. There is no allowance for dialogue and clarifications between parties, or adjustments to be made. Thus, it is very important to be as clear and careful as possible.

Let Someone Else Read it

A solution I found to be very helpful, and one I strongly recommend, is to have someone else read your letters, memos and materials *before* you put them out. Make sure it is someone who is not afraid to give you an honest opinion. Otherwise, you are wasting your time and theirs. If you dictate to a clerical person, tell her/him that you want an opinion. Particularly, they should red flag anything that might be misinterpreted or create an unintended negative message. Just a simple, "Is this what you really want to say?" from your assistant can help you refocus and review your statements. Setting the document aside for a day also pays off in fewer needs for retractions, follow-up explanations, or the need to extract your foot from your mouth.

This goes along with one of the themes expressed throughout this material, that it is wise to solicit the ideas and opinions of others. Of course, these requests must be authentic and used where appropriate. You may have super great ideas, more experience and training, and know where you are going. If you operate from that mode, however, you will limit yourself and the organization; your eyes may be good, but they don't see what others may see. Equally important, or perhaps more important, in maximizing the potential of others, if you direct all the traffic and make all the decisions, you will not get the dedication and effort from the others that helps them grow, and helps your organization succeed.

Change Activity 37

You may believe that within your organization, you have the best communication system ever devised. Great! Then you certainly won't have a problem asking your people for their confirmation of that fact. And, who knows, maybe you missed something. If you follow through, at the very least, providing the next activity to your group will be another step in illustrating your value of them. This is an opportunity to pick up ideas and opinions and to get the staff more focused and supportive of your efforts.

Submit to your staff, employees, or workers, this simple questionnaire. It should be returned anonymously.

_____1. On a scale of 1-10 (ten being high and 1 being low) how do you rate overall communications in this organization?

_____2. How much could communications actually be improved.(1 to 10).

3. If you believe communications could be improved, please make suggestions.

Application

1. After you have compiled the information from the questionnaire, have a meeting with the group or groups and review with them what you have learned. In relation to what has been written, ask them to discuss the information and offer possible modification in communication.

2. After you have received the additional input, discussed it, and developed the best approach for implementation, use it. If it means emphasizing an approach, do it. If it means a significant change, develop a plan for implementation. The more people are a part of this, the more it will be followed. The more driven they are to implement anything, the more successful will be the operation, and the more successful will be the organization and you.

Consider (to yourself) Before You Leap

I talk to myself. I read aloud what I write. That all may sound vain and others might wonder. However, frequently the mere act of reading audibly something I have written or talking through a presentation I am about to make, reveals mistakes and confusing statements. And, by the way, talking to oneself is a practice some of the greatest minds have used. Another big advantage has to do with the fact that although you may be able to clarify, you cannot actually take back what you have said or written. Thus, it is important to use every device possible to ensure you convey what you want to convey. Anything else is not *effective* communication. Which leads us to the next topic.

No One Knows What You Think, Only What You Say

Sometimes in or after a dispute, the comment is made, "Do you think I can read your mind?" In a way, communication is a way of reading someone else's mind. And sometimes it would help communications considerably if people really could. However, there is another side to that.

If people could read our minds we would probably be in more trouble than we are under the current system. It is difficult not to have opinions about people. Sometimes our thoughts are perfectly rational and appropriate. At other times or in other situations, they may be negative, even bigoted. Some of these opinions are merely passing thoughts. Some of them are inconsequential. Others may be significant. The positive side of people not being able to read our mind, is that it allows us to review and make alterations as appropriate, with the result that what we say and write is more intentional. Some people use this fact to stay out of trouble; some do not.

A good example of not using that advantage surfaced in a court case a few years ago—*Price Waterhouse vs. Hopkins.*[32] In this situation, a female worker wanted to be considered for a partner position in an accounting firm. She was not given the position. In her evaluations there were negative comments tied to her gender: "walk more femininely," "talk more femininely…" These obviously were inappropriate statements, and the firm paid for that mistake.

In addition to the responsibility of leaders to be aware of what is and what is not legal, it is prudent that we do not make written or oral comments that are inappropriate. No one knows what you think until you share it. All of the apologies and retractions cannot erase the impression or information spoken or written. I am not encouraging negative thoughts nor having open and frank discussions as appropriate. I am advocating that you use the old saying: think before you leap. Each of us has total power over what we say, write, or do; use it.

Combining Direct and Indirect

To review, face-to-face, direct communication is effective in that it allows for vocal dynamics and body expression. It also conveys a feeling of importance to the issue and to the individual or individuals with whom you are meeting, and allows response and clarification. These are important in effective, maximizing leadership. This mode also has its limitations. Visual and auditory presentations are subject to interpretations. Thus, we can send confusing or even conflicting messages. Additionally, some people do not retain information presented in this manner.

Written communication, on the other hand, can provide detailed information that can be read and re-read. Thus, instructions, items, and procedures may be more clear. We say *may*, because written communication can also solidify impressions not wanted. The reader will interpret what he or she reads from an individual frame of reference; it may not be read and understood as it was written and intended. Also, the receiver may have only that material from which to make a judgment or decision without the opportunity, or in some cases, the inclination to check with the writer; misinformation can result. For example, one manager always put notes in the worker's mail slots. Those notes always said simply, "See Me." The only other information was his signature at the bottom. Employees who received their first note or two would go to his office with smiles on their faces. However, it did not take long to learn that almost all of the meetings were negative. Yet there were times when he had something positive to say. Unfortunately, when a note appeared in the mail room without any explanation, just the usual "See Me" message, negative assumptions prevailed.

A third mode of communicating, particularly in organizations, is to have a summary sheet of what you are saying that is quickly reviewed while you are saying it. Some organizations use an agenda. The limitations of an agenda, however, are that the topics may not provide details. People tend to write comments or notes to themselves on the agenda. Depending on the accuracy of the listener, these notes may or may not be complete or accurate.

My recommendation for group meetings and group understanding is to provide to each individual a written outline that includes the agenda topic headings and also short statements that include any special information, dates, related previous decisions, lists, anticipated questions that need to be answered, and assignments expected. Each item may be discussed briefly or extensively, and questions may be asked as appropriate. This makes follow-up easy and efficient. In a group meeting, this takes care of detailed information as well as face-to-face clarification. It also cuts total meeting time considerably.

Change Activity 38

Let us take a moment here and apply what we have discussed. How effective is the communication in your meetings? Having sat through meetings that seemed to go on and on and accomplish little, and having led many meetings, I have often wondered if my meetings were like the ones that people wished would get over. Does my staff dread getting together with me and would prefer not to have to attend? When they leave, do they feel the time has been well spent and helpful?

As leaders in the improvement process, we have to be able to look at ourselves and what we do. We have to be willing to take the scary step of looking into the mirror. There are two good ways to do this: (1) be the fly on the wall; (2) ask. In this exercise let us be the fly on the wall. Use either a video or audiotape machine. The video is better, but the alternative will do. Have someone who is not part of the meeting be responsible for making the records. Let that individual pick the meetings—and I suggest taping more than one. They need to be unobtrusive. They don't need to let you know when they are going to tape. You need to explain to the people with whom you meet what you are trying to do, and that from time to time the meetings will be taped for your benefit. As an aside, sharing with your people what was just suggested will, in itself, improve your standing and their attention. As participants, we are more likely to support individuals who believe they are human and are striving to improve than we are those who act as if they know it all.

In anticipation of the recording, you will probably find yourself preparing better meetings. Although that may seem to be kind of cheating, if it is moving you toward better meetings, you are already taking the desired steps. After all, improvement is not usually something that comes in a blazing fit of inspiration. Most often, it is just a day by day continual refining focus.

Since step by step changes are the most probable solution, in subsequent meetings, review those improvement items and note the progress. View or listen to the tapes. Use the form on the next page to help you utilize what you see and/or hear.

Since we are often blind to some of our strengths and weaknesses, an added help is to ask someone whom you trust and who is not threatened—who is not afraid to say to you what he or she thinks—to sit in on the viewing/listening sessions and note what he/she sees.

Focus	Date & meeting	Date & meeting	Date & meeting
Positive aspects observed			
Less effective aspects observed			
Possible positive changes			
Changes selected for next meeting			

Communication and Accountability

Before we leave this chapter, let us spend a moment on one of the most potentially positive and negative aspects of communication in an organization—accountability. Time after time, I have experienced and witnessed the blame game. It usually goes something like this: "You never told me I was supposed to do that; it was not my responsibility!" or "If you would have listened to what I said!" or "I told you it would take longer than that!" or (put your own here; I'm sure you have some.) Unfortunately, most of these accountability-communication situations that come to mind are negative. The end result is misunderstandings, hurt feelings, disgruntled workers, poorer production, and even sabotage.

The most effective way to unscramble this egg is to combine direct and indirect and make sure that sincerity is in the mix. It is very important that you deal face to face with items, assignments or issues that are not routine, or with individuals who often seem not to understand, have a history of not being accountable or who seem to be involved most frequently in the blame game. Face to face discussion often reveals areas overlooked or that might be overlooked in the process. It also allows misunderstandings to be discussed and determinations of responsibility to be finalized. If leadership is open to listening and allows, or better yet, invites differences to be discussed, these meetings will be rewarding for everyone. On the other hand if, unfortunately, leadership is just into telling, using direct and indirect methods will still be the most productive.

In my experience, there are a lot of these meetings that fail to capitalize on the process because they do not take the indirect step. They fail to write things down.

The most effective process is to (1) meet together, work out the process, assignments, timelines and responsibilities; (2) record these decisions in writing; (3) review them as a summary of the meeting with the individual or group; and (4) provide a follow up copy or e-mail to everyone involved. As a result, it is easy to follow the progress, see who needs help, and make adjustments as needed. It also minimizes the personal disputes while focusing on the goal or task. Everyone is accountable.

So, let us quit talking and start operating. The most important place to start is with those with whom you always seem to be involved in one of the blame game dialogues.

Change Activity 39

This protocol is merely a recommendation. That is, it has the necessary parts to assist you in communicating and determining accountability. Like all of the exercises in this book, it should be adapted to fit your needs. A caution: if your goal is to improve the bottom line—your people—and ultimately the total operation, do not take the previous statement as an excuse to slide over this. Remember one of our themes throughout this book is that almost every choice in life is optional; the consequences of the choices, however, are not.

1. General description of project, goal, or concern:

_____

_____

_____

_____

2. Components required to successfully and optimally complete the project or goal, or resolve the concern:

_____

_____

_____

_____

3. Individual responsible for each component:

_____

_____

_____

_____

4. Completion date of each component:

_____

_____

_____

_____

5. Description of appropriate item completion; what is required for a satisfactory completion:

_____

_____

_____

_____

6. Additional comments or understandings:

_____

_____

_____

_____

Summary

This chapter was started with quotes from leaders noting the importance of communication. Since that introduction, I have spent your time attempting to make more apparent the importance of the nuances in communication. These are things that make the difference between communication and effective communication. To some, this may seem like overkill and unnecessary. Unfortunately, that attitude can be a strong indicator of a significant problem. Unfortunately, these leaders will never get maximum effort from their people. Most businesses would be pleased if I could tell them how to get another five to ten percent gain. I am! Effective communication is a foundation that supports a structure that will do that.

10

MAKING CHANGES

Visionary leaders and change agents see beyond the immediate discomfort to the bigger payoffs.[33]

—Thomas A. Kayser

The Difference That Makes the Difference

Sometimes, our logical thinking gets sidetracked. Because there are always problems, we get into a problem-solving mode. It is not that problems do not need to be solved; if the boiler blows up, it cannot just be forgotten or a sticky note placed on the office door reminding us to deal with it next month. On a tough Monday morning solving all of the problems presented may seem like reaching the summit of Everest. But, as I have already stated, and as Robert Fritz in his book *The Path of Least Resistance* notes: solving problems only results in no problems.[34] That statement may stop you for a moment. Perhaps your next thought is, "Wouldn't that be wonderful!" That, however, is like a golfer after a hard day on the course being elated because he kept the ball out of the rough, or a skier feeling great satisfaction that she got down the hill without breaking her leg. Both are accomplishments. But they are pretty limited accomplishments. Both are only freedom from a negative situation. If, however, that is the way you think in your organization, if that is the kind of leadership you are providing, you may want to get a second opinion. Solving problems can be considered another wrong bottom line. Remember, the goal is *optimal* accomplishment.

It should be common knowledge that maximizing potential is more than solving problems. President Kennedy did not say before the end of the decade we would get our rockets off the ground, which after the numerous failures, would not have been a bad statement. He said that we would have a man on the moon. That, at the time was one tall order. He applied a principle that we have already mentioned and is essential for developing people and improving organizations: the future dictates the present.

If we are to advance, we must see things as they could be or ought to be. Consider the concept of Disneyland, Disney World, and Epcot Center. I have often thought about Walt Disney and what he did. I could imagine some guy coming to my bank, wanting millions of dollars to erect amusement parks, carnivals with rides and people running around in costumes. What would I have thought if he would have said that someday there would be several of these, and that they would gross billions! With my limited vision, I would have tried to talk him out of such an unlikely and absurd venture.

We are affected by what we see and what we have seen—what we are familiar with. This is where our short-sighted logic gets us into trouble. As we have already discussed in this book, we see what we expect to see. We are often confined to our own box, not by someone else, but by ourselves. And in fact, even when we really know we should get out of the box, sometimes we choose to stay.

Of course, in truth, we do change. We get older. We have new experiences. As we witness the world's happenings and developments, we cannot keep from being aware and being affected. The important questions then are how are we changing and how fast. In his book *Fourth Generation Management,*[35] Brian Joiner notes that in his discussions with managers, he asked them if they were improving. The answer was always yes. The next, and most important question he asked was if they were improving fast enough. As we look around we see many organizations changing. But in today's world, we see changes and improvements happening at a dizzying rate. Kodak, long the name associated with pictures, film, and cameras and a business responsible for well over 130,000 jobs, found itself behind the change curve. Leadership's failure to move rapidly enough into the digital world contributed to cutting the number of employees in half. Effective change is often like jumping a crevasse: a great effort that gets you 95% of the way across is not good enough.

Although most leaders embrace the need for improvement, it is sometimes difficult to find those active enough in the process—particularly in making changes that directly affect personnel. Developing an atmosphere where people resources are optimized can be very inexpensive yet provide significant returns. So, why don't changes happen more often?

Reasons Changes Do Not Happen

First is ignorance, disbelief, or not understanding what really matters to individuals. There are those leaders who do not believe there is a concern by workers in their organization and, because of that thinking, fail to pay attention. At the very least, it would be prudent to do some careful examination. This is a key. That is why there are so many exercises throughout this book dedicated to helping you examine your view of reality. You need to make sure it *is* reality.

Second, there are those leaders who tend to be trend followers, yet do not have a deep enough understanding of the concepts involved or a strong enough commitment to be successful. They read, attend seminars and conventions, and believe that the ideas apply to their organization. Their attention and intentions are commendable—they want positive change. Their practice, however, can be detrimental.

For example, the leadership of a certain business quotes to its employees from one of the leading business writers. They talk about following the philosophy. They encourage all employees to become familiar with the ideas and demonstrate them in their work. The company's continuing operation shows, however, that they reward and promote those individuals who illustrate a different philosophy. The result is continual turmoil. My discussion with their employees revealed a more hostile feeling created by the incongruity than by their poor practices.

Another problem that can materialize from this situation, and that will thwart effective change, is if leadership becomes aware of the feelings of the employees. Leadership may tend to believe that their efforts are not appreciated and not worth the trouble. It sometimes justifies a belief that they are better off staying with what they have been doing. It can even turn into an emotional hurt, as it were, "we make all of these efforts and no one appreciates them!" This can diminish the probability of future change efforts.

Meaningful change takes time. The line workers have to experience a continual practice before they will trust. They must trust before they will be supportive and truly involved. Although some support can be expected immediately, in my experience, it takes a significant period of consistent practice, particularly by leadership, before the rank and file are willing to seriously invest. That is another reason why this book is full of exercises. They are designed to keep you moving—not to take one shot and decide that is enough, or that things will not work.

Third, there are those who become zealots and believe they can force their newfound religion, as it were, on the staff. This is a very difficult spot to be in. It can be very frustrating. You have determined a direction you strongly believe will make a positive difference. You have seen a new light. You are excited. There are examples of other places it has worked. You can visualize the expected improvements. And you may be correct. You may have located concepts or practices that will revolutionize the organization. However, excellence cannot be forced. It ties into motivation; the key to that door is on the inside. Motivation is not something you do to others; it is something they do to themselves.

In my experience, the most successful improvements have come through *infecting* rather than forcing. Particularly in a larger organization, this has worked well. Find a unit or facet of the organization willing to try the ideas. After some success is produced, provide opportunities for them to share and promote with others. The result is a larger and larger group of supporters instead of saboteurs. Additionally, this builds trust in the leadership and greater self-confidence and productivity in personnel. It becomes theirs, and they won't want it to fail.

Fourth, there are those who attempt to teach the process, but do not have the expertise. They come away from a presentation with information. They are enthused about the possibilities. They see the advantages. However, in most of us, what we learn tends to decay very rapidly. And what we don't know, we can't teach. We may not have complete enough information. We may have limited skills. We may have not had experience in presenting the idea. Bringing a program or process to fruition usually takes a very complete understanding and/or experience with it. Otherwise, it is much like telling a joke when you cannot quite remember all the parts or the punch line. It has little impact.

In this book, I have taken a step around that problem. The activities provided are designed to be easy for anyone. They do require attention and sincerity, but not formal training. The idea of all of them is to develop a mindset and an opportunity to practice more effective processes. After you have been successful, you can share some of the processes with other supervisory people.

<u>Fifth, there are those who just want what they want.</u> Although most leaders generally believe in the McGregor X/Y idea that people are inherently positive and they want the best for everyone, I have run into some leaders who were extremely negative and seemingly just wanted what they wanted even if it meant inflicting pain and not reaching rational goals. Whether it came from some background experiences that left resentment, was a quirk of nature, a manifestation of insecurity, or from some other unseen power, I do not know. I do know that nothing seemed to move them from their locked state of mind. They would not change. Unfortunately, the spots in which they were cemented were not helpful to other leaders, workers, the organization or even themselves. In this situation, significant people development is not possible. In my experience, they may verbally endorse a positive movement that will help people and the organization, but will undermine it.

It is my hope, that if you are one of these individuals, you will take a couple of steps back, look in the mirror and see who you want to be. My promise is that you will get some of the results you desire by modifying your approach and you will enjoy what you do more.

<u>Lastly, there are those who demonstrate a seeming lack of integrity.</u> At least, that is how the rank and file perceive them. Sometimes this comes from leaders who truly want the best, talk the best, but cannot quite manage the real application. Like dieting or the cessation of smoking. It is easier to talk about it than to do it. This frailty of human nature does not have to be perceived as lack of integrity. There are ways of working with others that will minimize that perception.

As leaders, we simply must illustrate our fidelity to what we profess. The result of incongruity and the dissonance it creates is much worse than if we operate in almost any other way. People can accept the sour individual (if you are a jerk, be a jerk). They can tolerate the trend follower. They may not become converted to the idea of the zealot, and they may excuse the ineptness of the leader who would teach what he or she does not know. But they revolt most against leadership they perceive as insincere and dishonest. In fact as I have already stated, this is the number one complaint I hear from line employees, middle management, teachers, bus drivers, custodians, paraprofessional, professionals, volunteers, and others. Let me repeat that concept. The most distasteful and destructive, the most counterproductive feeling found in workers is distrust of leadership. There must be an openness and consistency from leaders over a significant period of time that illustrates sincerity, honesty, and trust, to convince particularly those who have had bad experiences.

Of course you may be perceived as lacking integrity, but not be so. Assuming that you are in fact not one of the deceptive individuals, the great number of activities in this book are here to assist you in establishing practices that, if you consistently and sincerely carry them out, will illustrate your true colors.

As noted by the items above, change is tied to thinking. Change is directly connected to the beliefs and desires of those involved. Although many components have a bearing on change, such as industry, the market, economy, weather, or the world situation, they do not dictate how we operate within those situations.

This brings us back to the keystone of the arch—the critical element.

The Most Difficult Object to Change

We often look at the people at work, at home, at meetings, and in the world as our difficulty. It just seems they will not change. I once lived in the same community as one of my uncles and his mother (my grandmother). My uncle did a lot of things for my grandmother. And a number of times he commented in a loving way, "Oh mother, you are getting a little picky and difficult." I recall a time when his mother responded with, "Not as bad as you will be when you are my age." Of course, he took that in a loving way and they both laughed. And, of course, she was right; he was certainly no less fussy in his later age. Which brings us to this topic of change.

All of the things I have talked about in this book assume that there is an interest in learning and making change. I was once taught that the word *assumption* was a very weak word. Nevertheless, I *assume* you have better things to do with your time than to read things that are of no value, things that you do not believe in, things to which you will pay no attention. I assume you would like to improve what you do and how you do it. I believe you want your organization to be more effective, make more money, have a greater market share, score higher, or whatever. So let us come to grips as individuals with a couple of our most formidable challenges: (1) changing ourselves, and (2) realizing that change is tied not only into what we do, but who we are.

Change Is Difficult

The difficulty of change and particularly, changing ourselves, is a real barrier. Sometimes we operate as if we need only to read and learn, and the improvements and changes will happen; they will somehow appear. That brings us back to the theme of my organization, *Applied Focus*. That is not merely the title of an organization; it is an action commitment. To be successful, we need to know where we are going, have ideas, concepts and objectives upon which we can *focus*. However, that is not enough. We have to put into motion a process targeting that focus. We must *apply* what we know and believe before it makes a difference.

While we sometimes absorb ideas that filter into how we operate, significant change takes thought, planning and work. Actually, if merely accepting an idea brought about change, the world would be considerably different. There would be few weight-loss methods, few finance counselors, few wreckers and body shops, fewer medical bills, and even fewer deaths. After all, if everyone who wanted to lose weight or get fit was able to meet their desire, there would be a lot of appropriately fit folks. It would be that simple! Look around; that is not the case. Why?

For most of us, it is just not that easy. We know why we should do it. We have a desire to do it. We know how to do it. We have the means to do it. We may even start to work at it for a time. Then there is a breakdown. That failure point is responsible for the dissatisfaction in the workplace. Of course, everything is not so simple to analyze nor as one-sided. This problem of individuals is also reflected in groups.

This phenomenon is not just a business problem. It is everywhere. An education establishment worked for two years using a model of total representation by students, teachers, administrators, community leaders, parents and board members. Hours and hours of work were donated. Significant plans were begun. Then, unilaterally, the board made a series of decisions 180 degrees from the movement. There was little regard for the process or respect for those individuals who had been involved. Staff and community were, and will continue to be, significantly disturbed. The result, instead of improvements, positive changes and greater success, were a decline in support and trust.

Challenge two is even more profound: understanding that change is the modification of what we are. It is not something out there, but inside. One of the themes I have repeatedly emphasized throughout our discussions is being real. Pretension can be a form of dishonesty—we act like something we are not. However, to make a change, we must *almost* pretend. That is, we have to do things differently. We have to walk to the edge of the light, as one person noted. Or in the words of Shakespeare in the third act of *Hamlet,* "Assume a virtue, if you have it not." This is not counterfeit.

Change usually requires us to take a stance that is not quite us, so to speak. If I want to be the world's greatest batter, regardless of what I know, sometime or other I must swing at the ball. To be a better leader, I must step up and swing at the ball—act like a better leader. I must treat people as the better leader would. That usually takes moving to the edge of our comfort zone. It may not feel like you. That is not only acceptable in change, it is necessary. When you first learned to drive a car, your actions were probably somewhat jerky, your mind was working hard, and your eyes were anxiously scanning all around. This new experience required, even demanded, significant effort. I remember well learning to drive; I am sure my father did too. Our car had a clutch and conventional gearing. My father spent a number of hours and days with me on an abandoned street. I would put one foot on the clutch and the other on the gas. I would slowly let out the clutch while trying to coordinate an increase on the accelerator. In the beginning, things were pretty jerky. Eventually, I got the hang of it. In fact, today I drive a car with a clutch, yet I move quickly, effectively and smoothly through the gears, with little or no thought.

The point: at first, attempting to be the leader you would like to be and employing the approaches you would like to use, is uncomfortable, difficult and awkward. It may be looked upon by others with unsurity. Your sincerity will be a key to their acceptance of you, and your blunders and awkwardness. If you are sincere and persistent, you will move from merely *doing*, to *being*. As scary as it sounds, that is really the goal. The transformation will not only be in your organization and around you, it will be *you*.

Change Activity 40

Throughout these chapters you have been asked to consider and do many things. These were change activities. I do not know how faithfully you have done what was asked. I do not know how successful you have been to this point. However, often we fail to realize our progress until we look back. Like a mountaineer, we need to stop and look at where we came from. That is very important. It is important because that perspective can provide the energy to continue. So, instead of having you do some change activity, I want you to do an activity that helps you see the progress you have made. It is a time to evaluate and pat yourself on the back. It is not a time to get picky or find fault with yourself.

If you have not participated, hopefully by now you will have perceived where we are going, why we are going, and have a desire to go there. Go back and try some exercises.

As you evaluate, you will most likely see some areas that are not where you want them. But just for this time, let us focus only on the growth. In fact, let me fill in the first one.

Progress I Have Made

I am reading this book about focusing on developing me to be a more effective catalyst in helping my people and my organization to be optimally successful.

Application

Hopefully in the activity you just completed, you have noted efforts and acknowledged yourself. If you have taken the message of this book and seriously pursued it through the activities provided, there should have been some movement. There should have been some changes in the people with whom you deal and the organization. Maybe you have seen changes in you.

If, however, you are like most of us, there are areas that need more work—that you skimmed over or do not like to deal with, think not very important, or just did not find success. Be careful. Often some of our greatest needs are those we think we have under full control. Your assignment is to pick some area you honestly do not like or have had a problem with, and either devise your own approach or use one in the book. Note it below.

An area in which I could use further work:

_____

_____

_____

_____

What I will do to improve my performance in that area:

_____

_____

_____

_____

_____

11

PLANNING, GOALS AND MEETINGS

A Process Not a Program

The basic format for this book is built around the development of personal skills that form a substructure upon which your everyday decisions, organizational policies, procedures, and overall organization can operate, and that maximize your most critically important asset, people. Thus, this chapter may seem a bit out of place. However, the process of determining direction and planning a course to achieve those goals is logically and personally important. Attention to important principles and keys to effective planning form the foundation for your success as a leader.

There are virtually no goals of which I am aware that are terminal—that do not produce a need to move on to more goals. In work, we sometimes visualize the perfect position, the right salary, the best benefits. Starting out many years ago, fresh out of college and single, I knew of people making a thousand dollars a month. My thought at that time was, "How could anyone need any more?" Of course, by today's United States' standards, that is a poverty income. Beginning college, it was a dream to finish a B.S. and actually have a college degree. Much time and education past that, I found myself with degrees beyond. I once viewed a particular administrative position in a certain-sized organization with awe. Only super individuals were in those spots, I thought. A few years later, I held that coveted position in an even larger organization. I was no glorified being, and as I looked around at comrades at similar levels, I noticed they seemed to be just normal humans, too. When we were first married, one of my wife's lamentation themes was that she would never be blessed to have a child. Five boys and two girls later, she had to throw that one out. I could go on; you could go on—having a bicycle, driving a car, learning to swim, catching a fish, getting married, having a child, having a home. Going to school is the pre-schooler's goal, getting out is the teenager's. It does not matter whether we are talking about domestics, work, skills, sports, money, or whatever. The fact remains that as we reach the top of one hill, we discover several others beyond.

Goals, then, are not terminal. They are merely steps on a path. Although there are turns beyond what we can see from our vantage point, the path leads on and on. Since we are not always able to anticipate the direction, we need to be ready and capable of adjusting our bearing. We need to be able to modify or even throw out past goals.

Leaders understand that goals are part of a dynamic process. Successful leaders are able to modify and change goals as needed. The most successful leaders are those who look for changes and anticipate the need to modify goals. Unsuccessful leaders tend to be entrenched and paralyzed by their own paradigms; they see goals as terminal. With their limited vision of existence, they see *their* mountain as the highest peak. They often do not think of the whole earth, seldom the solar system, almost never the universe. This concept is perhaps the most important to our success, since it keeps all possibilities open to us.

Let me step back for a moment and add a qualifier to these previous statements. There are a few terminal goals that may never change. For example, a school district has as its mission, its end goal, the success of each child. That kind of end result could always stand with little argument. However, the definition of *success* may be revisited. The sub-goals on how to get to that ultimate quest will be in continual review. And finally, while the focus may always stay the same, in application the actual achievement will always be an unobtainable peak.

Successful leaders understand the concept of synergy, that the result is greater than the sum. This is one of the main themes of this book. The most successful leaders know that by utilizing the visions of others and coupling them with their own, the journey will be more productive. If, as I encourage, they keep in mind the humanistic view of building others, the results will expand exponentially. In fact, the success of the activity will be in direct proportion to the involvement and growth of the individuals. It might be illustrated: NIG=LOS (Number of Individuals Gaining = Level of Organizational Success). That is hardly $E=MC^2$. However, the end result may not be far behind.

Change Activity 41

To help you more clearly differentiate between mission goals that may forever stay the same and process goals that may change, and to determine if the professed goals are the practiced ones, take a moment, pick some organizations or businesses and complete the form below. In your list, make sure to include your own organization. If there are no established goals, look at the operation and see what overall mission or goals are *implied* by the way things are done and the emphasis placed.

All people and organizations have goals. They sometimes do not profess them. They sometimes do not even recognize them. Yet the very lack of a goal is part of their goals, professed or not. It is enlightening, even fun, to attempt to determine the goals of organizations by what they actually do, then contrast that with what they say their goals are.

1.   In the first column write the main mission or goal.
2.   In the second column, boil that down; what does it really say?
3.   Review how the organization operates. If the operation closely matches the main stated mission, note that in column three. If it does not, in column three note the apparent underlying goal or mission.

1. Mission and/or professed goals.	2. Define what that seems to mean.	3. Note the actual, demonstrated goals.

If you did Activity 41 conscientiously, you should have a picture of what your organization professes and how it actually operates. Of course, you realize that this is your opinion. One of the problems that I continually see in organizations is that everyone walks around with their opinion and the assumption that things are as they perceive them. While your opinion is important, it is as important or perhaps more important to know how others view the operation. Some leaders do not like to hear what others think. Of course that is a significant ingredient in mediocrity and failure. It is far better to know what others think even if you feel you cannot modify your direction. Remember that regardless of whether you know or not, it is still there. It is as one psychologist used to refer to as the elephant in the living room. That is, there is something there, everyone knows it is there, but no one wants to accept the fact and deal with it.

Change Activity 42

Take that same exercise (number 41) and do it with your leadership team or supervisors. It is not necessary for you to share your original determinations. In fact, it is better if you don't. Unfortunately, too often middle managers are used to echoing the boss's lead. In some situations they find that much safer. Hopefully, that is not the way they feel in your organization. However, if it is, it is. That is a good point to start from. Just a note, this same exercise can be done by supervisors with those supervised, with customers, even in families. It is not just useful for the CEO. Try not to lead your subordinates into your opinion. You may want someone else to actually run the session. One caution: you are not doing this to criticize other businesses or organizations. Be careful that this does not get into a bashing activity. You merely discover what you discover.

Application

Take a variation of this to the total organization as part of the process of growth and improvement. I suggest that you use a couple of examples that came from Activity 42 to illustrate what you are doing. Share with your people the theme that if we want to move effectively and efficiently, we really have to define as well as possible our main function, goal or quest. Then have them examine your organization.

Have fun with this. Call it something like "Life as it is." Encourage openness. If it helps, have them take the form back to their areas of work and complete it. They can then return it to a designated individual who will compile them.

I recommend an additional step. After you have the information they have shared, spend some direct time with them reviewing the information and encouraging comments and recommendations.

At the end of Activity 41 and the Application, you should have a more accurate picture of what your group really believes your organization stands for. That is an important stepping off place for an organization's self-evaluation. It is a necessary step. It can be uncomfortable to discover that what you profess is not your functioning focus and that something else, perhaps less desirable or noble, is. If you are concerned about doing this that could be a clue that perhaps you should be. If you, and your group are going to approach your capability, it is a necessary step.

Some of us do not feel comfortable with growing older and looking older. Although I may maintain the rigors of many activities and do my best to look young, upon looking in the mirror and reviewing pictures of me twenty years ago, there is no denying I am older and I am looking older. Whatever the desired truth, this *is* the truth. Although it may not be what I want, this understanding is not only okay, it is helpful. It may even keep me out of trouble. Your organization is the same. Being real is appropriate and helpful. Pretending is a waste of time and restricts progress. And knowing still allows choices.

Of course, having a clear picture does not mandate change. There is a business that produces on a limited basis. The middle managers would like to see expansion into the market that is readily available.

The owner likes the business the way it is. It is prospering and meeting the needs he has. It is his business. He is not pretending; he just wants it to stay as it is. There is no law that says he must enlarge or modify it. This is so in your situation. It can be very helpful, however, to see the total picture.

Having a clear picture helps us make better choices, or at least see the probable outcome. But, as I noted above, *knowing* possibilities and probabilities in no way forces us to make different choices, just like visiting a car sales lot does not require us to buy a car. Knowing does help us predict the reality of those choices. In a small town, there was an individual who had been quite successful at running a theater. As part of his enterprise, he added an adjacent sandwich shop. That worked well for a while. Then, without really looking at his goals and appraising probabilities, he decided to make it a top-of-the-line ice cream shop that included actually making the ice cream. The cost of expensive equipment and supplies far surpassed revenue. Again, without stepping back and looking, without involving anyone else or developing a plan, he began supporting his shop with the profits from the theater. That brought an ultimate end to both enterprises.

A mall child-care center was opened. After about three months, it failed. The owner had determined a goal of providing the very best and safest place for children. Unfortunately, he should have examined more carefully the survival goal of making enough money to support the business. All his estimates of financial success were based on unrealistic projections.

For success, every organization has to determine (1) the real objective, and (2) how all the sub-objectives focus on that goal. That means that you as the leader must be willing to ask the hard question: is what we profess what we do, and do our actions support what we profess?

Change Activity 43

In the last activity, you examined the bottom line mission(s), the real mission, professed or not, of organizations. There should already be in place objectives and processes that facilitate reaching these ultimate goals. There also may be some processes and sub-goals that seem to have nothing to do with the espoused end results. For this exercise, a sub-goal would be a process or steps in a process, procedures, where money is spent, etc.

As a base line for moving forward:

1.   Make a quick list of the most apparent sub-goals and processes that are part of the organization.
2.   Note with a check mark, in your opinion, how they focus on the end goals or missions.

Sub-goal or process	very well	some	does not

Change Activity 44

To assist in getting an even clearer picture, do number 43 with your middle managers.

Application

Do Activity 43 with all your workers much as you did the previous activity. You may wish to read the next part before doing this.

Rules of the Road

Since you as a leader must be involved in the vision of the future and how to help others move in a productive direction to reach that view, it is important that you realize the driving forces with which you must deal to accomplish your objective. Let us review.

The pride that gets in the way of willingness to learn.

There is a little child in the highchair who, as she is attempting to feed herself, keeps missing her mouth with her spoon. You step in to help. After all, her objective is to eat. She wants the food. Yet in her efforts, she puts half of it on her face and another quarter down her front; only a small amount reaches the desired target. You want to help her get all of it into her mouth while, of course, also sparing you the agony of the mess. What could be better? You take the spoon from her messy little fist, fill it with the stuff from the bowl and attempt to direct it into her mouth. She turns her head! You try again; she hits the spoon with her hand. Is this logical, you ask yourself? After a few tries, you disgustedly put the spoon back down. She promptly picks it up and happily starts her low-percentage operation again.

You go to work. You find a memo on your desk stating that a certain program will be discontinued. In its place will be a new decision-making process. "What?" You exclaim. "How stupid!" The current program has worked for years! Along with the memo is a fact sheet showing graphs and statistics backing the change. Your thoughts are, "Sure, sure, and here we go again on another goose chase!"

It is more difficult to live with the decisions of others and take advice from others when the ideas are not ours or when we have not been involved. Almost everyone has experienced this resistance. The more the decision affects us, the stronger we feel. The perplexing part is that while everyone may accept this truism, commonly, we tend to operate as if it did not exist. When it comes to making decisions, we tend to forget or downplay it. In fact, sometimes when we are moving in a direction that affects others in the organization, we totally forget how we felt when someone tried to tell *us* what to do or to take over what *we* felt was the right way. Often, we get into the belief that our ideas are *the* ideas. Although it starts very young, it often does not evaporate with age. And unfortunately, in my experience, the group most likely to violate this principle is the one most resistant to ideas outside their own—leadership. Often, supervisors, administrators, boards, and CEOs are the most intractable.

You are the leader, superintendent, CEO, director, supervisor, principal, parent. I have presented you with ideas, exercises and recommendations. Are you openly reading and considering? Are you using the exercises to test the ideas? (Could it be that there is some baby food spilled on your shirt?) Of course, it is not like the baby; it is different. After all, we *know* how to be efficient and are open to suggestions…. or are we? At this point, some people are offended. Sorry. That is not my objective. I am only relating what I have seen and experienced.

Human beings want to grow. Dr. William Purkey, talking to educators, makes the statement that saying children don't want to learn is like saying acorns don't want to be oak trees. He adds that they may not want to learn *what* we want them to learn, *when* we want them to learn, or *how* we want them to learn, but they want to learn.[36] Every human being also wants to be empowered, to be able to make their own decisions and determine their own path. They want to be involved in making choices. They want to be successful. The messy child will eventually *develop,* which is a key word here, her ability to feed herself very efficiently and neatly, perhaps better than the individual who tried to feed her. However, you can't *develop* her. Just like the little child, an adult who is forced, pressured, threatened, or coerced will not be as supportive or successful, nor encourage others to be as supportive, helpful, or successful as one who has had the opportunity to provide input, be a part of the process, contribute, and develop an appreciation, and even a skill that evolves only through maximum involvement.

The total goal of this book is to help you be a leader who truly provides the opportunity and assistance for others to grow. Your task is to develop and empower people. I have promised, that like all gifts of greatest value, the more you give away, the more you have. I also stand behind the idea that if you focus on the correct bottom line—people—everything else will succeed at a higher level. On an organizational-type practical view, applying this principle will result in growth and success of your enterprise, and to a degree not possible any other way.

Throughout, what I have really been talking about is how decisions are made. So it is important that we share some specifics that will result in the greatest number of willing learners.

Rule #1: Involve the people, or bonafide representatives, who will be directly affected by the decisions.

Determine who should be involved in planning and setting goals by answering at least the following questions: Who will be directly affected? Who will be responsible for making the decisions work? Who would most likely have ideas that would be helpful? Who has expressed a desire to be part? Who needs to be aware? Who would not want to contribute? Include some of them, too. It is not recommended that you involve only those who agree with you. Of course, it is also advisable not to overload with those who disagree. Make sure that representatives from a group really are considered as such by that group—bonafide. It is often effective to ask the group to choose their representative. You can even use the sociogram provided in an earlier chapter. It helps you identify the *real* leaders from those who may merely have the title.

The degree of optimal success of the decisions will be directly proportional to the validity of the group making that decision. The validity of the group making the decision will be directly proportional to the way the total organization is represented.

Rule #2: Make everyone equal: level the playing field.

Get rid of rank. Rank can be very intimidating and stifle the development of some of the greatest ideas. This takes commitment, especially from leadership. We, as leaders, have to reverse our thinking and remember that without the line workers, the mechanics, the bus drivers—those that really get the job done—we would be unemployed. It also takes time. Frank, the guy who oils the rollers on the assembly line belt, will not usually feel comfortable freely expressing himself in the presence of his supervisor or the CEO. However, my experience has shown that the Franks of the world have many great ideas. Their involvement also makes a direct connection to a group of workers who do not often hold leadership in highest regard.

If it is explained to all involved that there is no rank, and that everyone is going by their first name, not Dr., boss, captain, or whatever, and if it is modeled, eventually the barriers will drop and people will talk like people. If this is a school district team, students ought to be involved, and if everyone is calling everyone by their first names, students should be part of the group. That goes for custodians, line workers, bag boys, or what have you. While being comfortable with this component will take time, it must be established and particularly exemplified by leadership; there can be no *others* in the group. If you are the chairman of the board and are not comfortable with the bag boy calling you Charlie instead of Mr. Big, or if you are Dr. Great, and wince when the custodian calls you Joe, practice alone in front of a mirror until the pain is not visible. Again the caution: regardless of whatever individuals say or do, you cannot assign consequences. One such incidence will drive the whole thing underground. As stated before, the negative results will be worse than if you never initiated the approach; if you are a jerk, be a jerk, but don't be a deceptive jerk.

Of course, if you cannot handle being one of the common folk, better not go this route, or send someone else. If getting rid of titles bothers you too much, you need to do a little self-examination. I agree with Yoda: unless you can operate within this realm, a great leader you will not be.

Rule #3: Put away the sacred dishes.

We often have visitors to our home. Our children come and bring their children. Since we do not have little children of our own anymore, there are in the home some things that are fascinating to look at, but easily broken. While we accept some rearrangement, breaking is not an end result we prefer. Thus, when we know there will be individuals who see and handle things in a different way than we do, we remove these objects from the scene. We can then relax, allow children to be children, and enjoy the visitors, small and large.

Although you will not normally be dealing with little children in your meetings, there will be those who might *break* or trample standards, traditions, or practices that you consider sacred. Indeed, the process of brainstorming encourages that kind of thing. Although I strongly urge you to be open to all ideas, if there are some things that at this stage in growth you hold and that you cannot or will not give up regardless of the thinking of others, do not put them on the table for dissection and possible destruction. Set the parameters of the process and the results at the outset. For example, if the focus is on improving communications, but telephone use has set parameters that you believe must stay, make that clear at the outset. Explain that your decision does not mean that this item could never be a focus of a group. It just means that it is not part of what you are about with this group at this time.

As I have already stated earlier, there is nothing that more quickly creates a problem than actions that are perceived as lacking integrity. Thus, having a group go into sacred territory, so to speak, and develop opinions and possible changes, only to come to a brick wall that says we are not going to do that, will destroy confidence in this and related processes.

There was an organization that went the strategic planning route. They went about every step in an exemplary manner. They involved representatives, leveled the playing field, truly paid attention to the recommendations, and developed a great process and reporting system. Then, in one swoop, without review or explanation, the governing group said "no." The result was a lot of behind the scene grumbling, mistrust, and underground discussions.

In another situation, a board of directors requested that a leadership team locate, review, interview and select an individual for a position in one of the organization's units. After a lengthy and time-consuming process, the team presented their choice. The directors would not accept the selection. The team members were extremely upset and refused to be involved in future processes.

If you as the leader will not tolerate giving up your parking spot, should it come up as a question, take it off the auction block with a short statement that you appreciate the desire of the group to have it there, but it is not something for consideration at the time. Although this will not set well with some, it is the best choice in relation to the results of the total process. It will be more palatable to the group than trying to go against them after a decision has been made.

Rule #4: Everyone participates

There is nothing quite as ineffective as to invite individuals to represent all factions of an organization, then not let them speak. Frequently, leadership people, as would seem appropriate, are used to leading. That is their responsibility. Most line workers are used to following and doing what they are told to do. That, too, would seem an appropriate mode. When you invite people from the ends of these poles, plus a bunch in the middle, it is easy for the pecking order to appear. I say *appear*, because it may not be the intention of leadership, for example, to dominate the process. In fact, however, it is the logical expectation of many of the people involved.

If we want to establish and maintain the integrity of the process, everyone must participate, whatever it takes. If it means getting everyone to provide their opinions by going around the group on each item, do it. If you break into subgroups, be sure that there is a cross-section of levels in each, and a process that ensures everyone will throw in their thoughts. Select chairs from the non-manager people. *Everyone* participates.

Rule #5: The right questions.

One of the keys to exceptional leadership and the development of others, and the best results, is tied not to the answers, but the questions. This is a challenge for leadership. I recommend spending some time prior to meeting with others to develop some critical questions. These will set the tone for the process. You do not have to do them alone. One of the first group exercises can be to elicit and develop important questions.

Rule #6: All ideas are okay.

There is nothing that will shut down input faster than putdowns. When we start sharing what we think is important, we make ourselves vulnerable. In effect, we lower our shields. All it takes is a couple of well-placed blows, and the shields come back up. Additionally, not only does it shut down the input from that individual, it also makes others leery. Resentment can crop up quickly as well. If you create a current of these emotions, the chances for success are seriously diminished. All ideas are okay for consideration. Of course, as the group works through them, some will be eliminated. In fact, in my experience, some of the people who suggested them will even lead in the elimination.

A special caution for leaders: When working in a mixed group of titled leaders and people who see themselves as merely workers, your expressed opinion and even your looks, can act as a put down. In other words, how you look and what you say means more than what someone else of lesser status says or does. This can be a tough assignment.

When I was a superintendent and knew I had a topic to present with which the board had strong negative feelings, or when I knew a very negatively aggressive group would address the board, I spent time with the board, and provided written instructions about such simple things that I had observed in members in the past, such as not paying attention to the speaker, talking among themselves, rolling their eyes, and negative noises or frowns.

In our group meetings, this problem is exacerbated by the habits and feelings within you. That is, you are used to having an opinion and making decisions. In a sense, once again, you will believe your ideas are the correct ideas. It may be difficult for you to hear ideas presented that you think are totally out of wack, and not be able to correct them. It may be hard for you to trust that the group will really come up with the best decisions. You may be very concerned that you feel as if you are giving away power, which, to some degree you are. You walk a tight line. Be aware and don't short circuit the process. Remember, your objective is just to be a member of the group. Do not think of everything as final or fatal. As difficult as it may be, try to listen as an uninvolved, unbiased listener.

Rule #7: Follow through.

While it is important to talk about things, it is critical to act on them. Because of past history, day to day disappointments, the realities of life, and whatever, when the boss says that the results of your involvement will result in positive changes, there is usually a tendency to be skeptical. We do not like to be disappointed. Especially if I perceive myself as a powerless worker, it is easier to assume the worst, that nothing really will come out of this, that leadership will pay no attention, that this is merely an exercise to placate us, that none of this will really change anything that happens to us; Monday morning it will be business as usual.

The actions revolving around the botched strategic planning situation previously noted is a good example that feeds this kind of thinking. All the platitudes and promises will not change this attitude. The only way to combat this way of thinking is proof: maintaining integrity.

If a decision is made by the group, it is acted on. If you as the leader do not like it, then you should not have asked the question. As noted in Rule #3, if there are areas that will not change, put them with the sacred dishes at the beginning of the process. Otherwise, there needs to be action. This is only logical. Going back to our *do unto other thinking,* how do you like to work on a project, spend time and effort, sincerely put out what you can, and then have someone erase the board and say, thanks? You can probably recall incidents that *smelled* like that. I use the emotional word *smell* to make a point. In those situations, the response is not merely a thought, but a feeling. Feelings have deeper, greater, and longer lasting impact.

Set parameters in the beginning so that any rational idea can be seriously pursued. On a positive note, although some of the ideas may sound bizarre, you will be surprised how effective they can be.

Rule #8: Be human and have fun.

That may sound strange: be human. Unfortunately, sometimes line workers do not see their supervisors, CEO and other leaders in a humanistic way. Sometimes your job may have a history of portraying you as a grouch, of seemingly disregarding workers as human beings, as the guy with the whip in one hand. Perhaps you have a reputation that appears to back that history. I am not throwing this out to judge. In fact, it really does not matter. You may recall our discussions about perception in a previous chapter. You could be the most congenial, warm human being on the planet. However, if Linda's only experience was a negative one, or if Fred heard you do not care about the guys in the maintenance shop, or even if your predecessor was the sour apple, that is their perception. And whatever they perceive is currently fact to them. So, be real. Be human. Have fun.

Smile, talk to them as people, not workers. A good practice might be to have a light lunch before the first meeting. Seat yourself in the middle of those who know you the *least*, and spend the time listening to them tell you about their families, their hobbies, and their thinking. Do not focus on you or the business. Get to know them as people. The greater the distance between your position and theirs, the greater the tendency for them to be conservative and hold back. The better they feel they know you, the more likely they are to honestly contribute and to respond to what they know. Your objective is to show that you view them as valuable human beings, not just as workers. Your objective is also to show them that you are also a human being, not just a boss.

You may find resistance. After taking over from a previous leader who was not well liked nor trusted, I made it a practice to attend meetings of different units. That allowed me to be just a bystander and get to know the people better. At the conclusion of one such meeting, I tried to come in contact with everyone by shaking their hands and listening to them. In response to my outstretched hand, one lady refused to take it. Although she did not know me at all—this was our first meeting—and I had been in the position for only a few weeks, she had strong feelings about leadership. My response to her was that I respected her feelings and that I hoped that at our next encounter she would feel differently.

Use humor. It is a great catalyst for relaxing people. I am not talking about a required joke at the beginning of each session. Find a way to be fun. As the leader, you can set the tone. In fact, the group will expect you to do that. This was your call. This was your invitation. They will look to you as a barometer on what they are doing, and for the feeling of the meetings. Make the meetings productive but also make them enjoyable. Try to be part of the group.

The one caveat in using humor has to do with sarcasm. Humor at the expense of others should be discouraged and avoided. A president who made a remark about sun glasses on a reporter later found out that the individual had a serious degenerative eye condition. What seemed funny at the time proved not to be. What you and others may think is funny, may not be to the individual about whom it revolves *even* though that person may laugh at it. Also, look out for sacred cows, as it were—gender related, music, blond jokes, etc. This is particularly important if you don't know the individuals in the group well. Not only do you not know what hurts them, but they may not know you well enough to tell when you are kidding or serious. When in doubt, don't.

Summary

Most of the ideas that were presented in this chapter are appropriate for staff meetings of any kind, and even with family and children; I immediately get on the floor with children. In my meetings with representatives from classified staff, I treat them just the same as I do upper mangers and professionals. Their job titles or assignments in no way change their importance and value as human beings; they appreciate it. If that is a problem for you, visit a hospital and a home for senior citizens. Recognize your humanness. Hopefully, you will gain a more real perspective.

We come into this world helpless and will probably go out helpless. In between we have for a short moment been given the opportunity to make a difference. Yes, we may have worked hard and earned that spot. However, at any point along the continuum, misfortune, disease, or any of a million things could have been different and resulted in a different situation. Remember, kings and presidents are people. Servants and street people are people. People are people.

Change Activity 45

You have probably noticed that we have just covered a lot of territory without a bunch of activities. That was done for two reasons. First, I do not want this book to be set aside because there just seems to be too many stops in it—places that you are supposed to do something. Second, because all of the concepts in this chapter are tied to one kind of process, they all need to be considered before they are used. But like any effective tool, these principles are *only* valuable if used. It is time to try them.

So let us get started. You may wish to start small. For example, if you are the CEO, meet with a representative (chosen by them) from the non-professional group. These would probably be custodians, maintenance people, maybe secretarial—if they seem to fit. Perhaps the topic could be improving communications between you and them. First, make sure you have some refreshments. Second, have each individual share some things about themselves and their lives. Of course, you participate as well. Third, be very attentive. Fourth, make sure that some action comes out of the meeting or meetings. And, by the way, merely by having the meetings you have already improved communications.

Let us summarize.

1. <u>Decide how extensive you wish this experience to be.</u> It could range from a small group dealing with a limited focus, to a department, or even representatives from all facets of the organization. It could be set up as a routine meeting or one that is to decide the ultimate direction of the enterprise, and that will require a significant time commitment from all involved.

2. <u>Decide the major focus or outcome expected</u>. Although one of the major reasons I encourage you to make this step is to build confidence in the system and your leadership, and to establish a conduit for ideas and improvements, there also needs to be an understanding by the participants of what you want to be the end result—the more tangible and quantifiable. Although this is an exercise, it must be much more.

3. <u>Use the following form to evaluate the process and the outcomes.</u>

Area of focus	Degree of accomplishment (date:)
#1: Involve the people or bonafide representatives who will be directly affected.	
#2: Make everyone equal; level the playing field.	
#3: Put away the sacred dishes.	
#4: Everyone participates.	
#5: The right questions.	
#6: All ideas are okay.	
#7: Follow through.	
#8: Be human and have fun.	

12

DIFFERENCES AND DISPUTES

Over the next generation, I predict society's greatest opportunities will lie in tapping human inclinations toward collaboration and compromise rather than stirring our proclivities for competition and rivalry. [These may be] the most creative social experiments of our time.[37]

—Derek C. Bok (President, Harvard University)

I have seen organizations, particularly small ones, purring along and, as long as there were no significant differences or major disasters, being successful. This is usually the picture of a new group. Everyone is focused on working together for the common goal. There is considerable unity of thought and purpose. However, as time passes and more individuals are involved, and more decisions made by new faces, misunderstandings and differences arise. Partners become contentious. Friendships become strained. Lines of command turn into struggles for power. I have previously discussed some reasons for those differences and made recommendations on how to avoid and/or minimize those situations. However, they can still happen.

When these differences rear their perplexing little heads, and they do, the tone changes considerably. These differences can be the turning point for the organization. Unfortunately, too many of these turns have been *down*. Some organizations never recover. Some do. Some leave scars and broken relationships that never heal. Others result in years of turmoil and mediocrity before regaining their effectiveness. Even when they survive, often there remains an undertone of mistrust that will ignite again given the right fuel. Thus, in my efforts to assist you in developing your people assets and optimizing your organization's effectiveness, it is appropriate to expose a stumbling block that can be merely a pebble today but a boulder tomorrow.

The Good, Bad and Ugly

Differences, like all choices, have a good side and a bad side. Without choices or differences, there would be much less contention. The absence of differences would result in the consumption of less time. We would not have to decide color, taste, model, or make. Purchasing a car, determining meals, looking for a home, choosing a flavor of ice cream, and working and living in harmony would be much easier. Meetings would be fewer and shorter. We would never be into the *who is right* fight because everyone would agree on what was right. Yes, life would be much easier.

On the other side of the coin, life without differences would also be incredibly bland, tasteless and stagnant. Living day after day in the same complete rut with everyone else would be mind-bogglingly dull. One of the greatest losses would be the lack of growth and learning, which is the excitement of life. Life without differences would be, in a sense, not living at all. Although we usually look at differences negatively, they are critical for advancement and survival.

Learning, growth and development are outgrowths of divergence and problems to be solved. Differences are the bedrock upon which stand choice. Choice is the essential component of growth. In fact, the advancements in society happen because of differences—people wanting to change something.

Differences are challenges to what each of us think or believe, or how we operate. After all, we each know that our way is the best way, toilet paper coming over the top of the roll, not the bottom; toothpaste squeezed from the bottom, not just anywhere on the tube. Differences are a bother that require thought and/or action. Dealing with varying opinions takes energy, takes time, takes effort.

It is very important that we look at differences as an okay part of the way people think, and not as an attack on our intelligence, our ideas, or even our authority, even when they may seem that way and may be presented in that atmosphere. Sometimes others are completely enveloped in the emotional facet of differences and thus become trapped in a corner surrounded by negative feelings and responses. However, it is our responsibility to turn these conflicts from lemons to lemonade. As a leader you have a responsibility to move outside that field. You must have a wider and more long-range vision. You must keep saying to yourself that differences are okay, even productive. It is important that we operate from that perspective because it clears our minds and our emotions, and allows us to look at the issues and the interests more clearly. That view facilitates better solutions, relationships and ultimately, productivity.

Change Activity 46

It is easy to read, nod in agreement then continue as usual. All of that is of little value if practices remain the same. Take a moment to pause, ponder and reflect, then do something; you and your organization will benefit. Remember that it is up you. If you do nothing, nothing will change, or in the phrase of the day, if you keep doing what you are doing, you will keep getting what you've got.

1. Quickly list differences that readily come to mind; I have provided some examples to give you a start.

2. Rate their current importance to you on a scale from 1 to 5 (5 is greatest in importance, 1 is least).

3. Rate their importance as you believe certain other individuals would rate them. If you haven't the faintest idea, guess based on your knowledge of the person.

4. Ask some of those individuals to rate some of these items. Don't tell them that you have rated them. Compare their answers with what you thought.

5. Duplicate this form with the issues you have added, and give to your group; it will not only prove very helpful in introducing a number of topics, it will be a fun way to start your meeting.

Issue	you	spouse	management /leadership	line workers	others—your choice use initials w/rating
direction toilet paper comes off the roll					
eating the cake so that the frosting is last					
hourly wage					
time clocks					
written contracts					
mission statements					
the organization's mission statement					
meeting efficiency					
the value of what we do in this organization					

You have just completed an exercise that helped you see a spectrum of differences. You found differences running on a scale and spanning a spectrum. On one end were mild, minor differences. Deciding, for example, to have lettuce or spinach in our salad, to wear the white or the tan shirt, the color of nail polish, to have the meeting Wednesday or Thursday, or how many blue pens to order, are all choices with differences that are pretty benign to at least most people. That, by the way, is a key point to remember. Something that is of little consequence to you may be a significant issue to others. In fact, you may have found something in the list above that I indicated were "benign" that are not to you. Generally, these are the types of things about which we have preferences, but are not emotionally, physically, or intellectually challenging. They are likely to pass by our mental guards and even our emotional guards, without much attention.

Moving up the spectrum toward the *red* as it were, the energy level increases. Emotional, mental, and sometimes physical demands are required. Here we begin to get closer to critical issues and to the core of the individual. For example, teaching methodology and classroom control, reasons for sales not keeping pace as predicted, who will be in charge of the project, how many employees to let go, the effectiveness of different individuals, organization policy, and organization practices, all start to draw more of our attention and energy. As the importance to our well being and our self-concept cranks in, the angle of importance steepens. The accompanying drain becomes more negatively synergistic.

Moving differences further up the scale into the dispute zone, we often find union negotiations, workers not performing, individuals undercutting, people attacking, grievances and lawsuits increasing, and strikes developing. With each step deeper into that zone, personnel alignment, emotional levels, stress, and negative feelings accelerate. As this happens, productivity, effectiveness, goal attainment, growth, and desire to serve drop off proportionally. Individuals and groups tend to pull up their walls, blame others, and progressively make it more difficult to move the lever in the opposite direction. The energy is put into a diving downward spiral. Once into this zone, not only can it destroy the organization, but also disrupt personal lives. Lasting negative feelings are spawned that can cripple the future. There are numerous examples. In fact, I see them every day. Let me just share a few.

The teacher's union was not happy with the financial package presented by the district board and administration. Some efforts were made to solve the problem, but to no avail. Staff began to line up against staff, community members against community members, students against students. As usually happens, everyone was blaming everyone else. A strike was called. After weeks of wrangling, a settlement was reached, people went back to work, and schools reopened. Although the staff was back working with kids, the turmoil had left serious scarring. A high school administrator who took a stand against the strike left the community. His comment several years later was that the negative feelings by many people within the community would never be reconciled. Some people who once called him a friend, now called him no more.

A manufacturing company found itself in a financial dilemma. They could not meet pay demands. The workers revolted. The company shut down. It has never opened again. It will never open again. The effect will be felt for at least a generation; feelings will persist for life.

A poorly handled dispute between an employee and a company eventually ended with a six digit settlement. It never needed to happen.

A group of staff members were asked to develop a project. They were empowered to make decisions and told they had full control. They spent many weeks of research and work in the endeavor, much on their own time. Upon completion, the governing power's response ranged from indifference to negativism. Illogically, they allowed an individual who had no connection with the project and little knowledge of the area under study to criticize and sidetrack progress. Feelings were hurt. Staff members were so upset that they determined they would not continue regardless of the consequences.

I could go on and on. In case after case, leadership did not deal with the situations in a productive way. True, there were many people who were involved and should have known better and done better. But when it comes to the final evaluation, leadership bears the weight. That is what leadership is all about. It is the responsibility of leaders to set the atmosphere and productively deal with differences and to provide the guidance and implement the actions that will result in success. *Productively* means that the best possible outcome will be *the* outcome. And that falls on the shoulders of leaders—CEO's, managers, supervisors, principals, foremen, presidents, superintendents, parents or anyone else who supervises others.

Styles

As already noted, differences are inevitable and essential for growth and improvement. In fact, if everyone is agreeing on everything, something may be wrong with the organization. Either you have hired a bunch of clones or you don't know what is really going on. Nevertheless, our objective as logical, productive and humanistic leaders is to use these differences as opportunities and make them as fruitful as possible. It is not always easy. Nevertheless, it is a challenge that comes with the territory. Of course, all differences will not end with "they lived happily ever after." Nor should they end with "not 'till Hell freezes over." A little common sense, coupled with understanding of what drives these humans, will give you a much higher percentage of *real* wins. Let us take a moment and view some frequently seen and simple profiles of leadership approaches.

First, there is the *father-knows-best.* In this mode the all-knowing leader provides the solutions, *period.* These people are easy to identify. They like autocratic assertiveness: "If you don't like the way we operate around here, don't let the door hit you on the way out!" That certainly is a way to handle differences. Unfortunately, this does not help people nor the organization grow and become more effective. It is not found in optimally successful organizations. The response I sometimes hear is "We are not here to baby sit people and help them grow; they should be full-grown when they come!" Of course you should be able to expect from everyone, competency and a certain understanding and support of the ideals and operation of the organization. However, if your attitude fits the statements at the first of this paragraph, perhaps you need to look in the mirror and determine who is not willing to grow. Checking the turnover rate and situation of people leaving may shed some light. Are more than the culls going out the door?

This leader type is one I see frequently, and often in leaders who deny its existence. If everyone in the organization is treated with the greatest respect, developed and empowered to make the best decisions, you, as the leader have an outstanding situation. In fact, the best possible. I have said it before, and will say it again: *organizations can only be as successful as the people involved. And the greater the percentage of successful people, the greater the success of the organization.* The added bonus is that the best, most capable, competent and intelligent human beings are attracted to these organization, and they are more likely to stay longer.

Organization can only be as successful as the people involved. And the greater the percentage of successful people, the greater the success of the organization.

The *father-knows-best* leaders believe they are doing their organization a favor by hiring and keeping what they consider as the no-nonsense, nose-to-the-grindstone, do-it-their-way, dedicated worker. In my experience of visiting, viewing, and working with organizations, not only do they not get the qualities they want and think they are getting, they never will. The best people will not work under that kind of leader. If they find themselves under one, they do not stay any longer than they have to.

Recently, for example, three different high-end skilled department leaders, individually and without my asking, expressed to me how dissatisfied they were with the company for which they worked. Their individual, but consistent complaints, focused around the lack of latitude, creative ideas, and optional decisions they were allowed to have and make. One has now left. The other two are looking. Repeated efforts to engage the CEO in a serious view of the situation have had no effect. Although a nice person in my experiences with him, his propensity to always know best provides added pounds of clutter that the organization must drag. An additional waste is that, feeling as the department leaders do, it is difficult for them to be optimally productive. Line workers in this same company have continually expressed dissatisfaction with their situation. Since this is a sizable organization, and my personal acquaintance with workers is limited, I suspect that there is a much greater problem than meets the eye.

The size of the organization has little to do with this situation. Two organizations, one large and the other very small, have the same problem and exhibit considerable turmoil. In one, the differences have been repeatedly expressed yet continually ignored. In the other, the employees are quiet and will not discuss the concerns. Their confiding in me was tied to my not identifying them. Leadership in this organization tends to reassign to less desirable positions those who are too divergent and vocal. These are just three examples. This is a problem that is pandemic in organizations across the spectrum.

Frankly, I do not consider the *father-knows-best* people as leaders at all. Much like the jailer, this style of leadership and handling problems is just a means of control. Although they may be great people with considerable skills, they stifle and stagnate. In our dynamic world there is no such thing as merely holding a place. We are either moving ahead, or the rest of the world is passing us by. Organizations run by *father-knows-best* will never attain what they could until they review their mode of operating with differences and make some changes.

At the other end of dispute resolution styles are the *don't-bother-me* managers. They may know that things are not going as they could and should, and that disputes are surfacing, but they just want everything to be solved. These well-meaning individuals are not fulfilling their stewardship. Confusion, negative feelings, lack of productivity, and stagnation will occur unless there are processes or methods to deal with the realities of organizations. Problems will not solve themselves.

For example, there is an organization that, as many do, started with outside financial backing. The plan was to pay back the loan over the period of three or more years. Instead, they were so successful, repayment was accelerated considerably. Additionally, prospects were great for larger and more lucrative accounts. Growth brought divergence. Leadership became fragmented, and differences, while not totally ignored, were not productively addressed. Ineffective processes were put into place to facilitate working through concerns. An efficiency analyst was hired. Unfortunately, he spent too much time looking at the wrong bottom lines and analyzing current statistics instead of looking over the hill and focusing on the people undercurrents. As a result, few changes were made and did not adequately solve the significant problems. As I began this book, the organization was on a downhill slide and the most competent and productive individuals were quietly looking elsewhere. I was concerned that there might be an unhappy ending. Unfortunately, as I write this, the company is no longer in existence.

In the realm of solving problems, being effective leaders, and focusing on the most important bottom line, these are examples of polar ends. Although these individuals and those not quite so polarized have the power to modify their thinking and operations, it is easier and more comfortable and convenient to stay with what they have. Additionally, and most detrimental, when approached, too often they refuse to accept the significant importance of making changes. They will probably ignore the fire until they are standing in the ashes.

There is another classification, and at whom this book is directed: those who see problems and are willing to look at themselves and their organization in hopes of making improvements. If you are one of those people, continue on. If you are not, you may want to consider continuing; your existence may count on it.

Change Activity 47

Sometimes we look at evaluations as negative. Like looking in the mirror, we often see things we do not particularly care for. Not looking, however, does not make them cease to exist. Unlike a physical image, the nice thing about our mode of operation is that it can be changed. Thus, these views can help us improve and become more effective in what we do, and in our lives, so that subsequent "looks" can be better. Actually, these evaluations are the only way we can improve. If we do not see any needs, we stay as we are.

In the following form quickly review leadership you have worked for, are aware of or who are part of your organization. Also, look at your own style. This is to assist you in being more able to focus and understand. These are also only generalizations to help you recognize *tendencies*. In fact, you may find folks who seem to operate from both ends. In those situation, try to determine their *favorite or usual* stance.

Individual (initial)	I will settle this thing!	I'm not getting involved	Review and collaborate	Give up. It can't be fixed
Me				

Application

1. Replicate the form you just used.
2. Without sharing what you did on your own, have leadership, partners, or supervisors do the same thing. They will not be required to share their work with their co-workers.
3. Use an example of a situation in which you were involved or that is outside your organization (it must not negatively reflect on them or their friends).
4. Discuss what happened positively and negatively, and imagine what the affect would have been under different approaches.
5. Of critical importance: how did the people in the organization or situation feel, or how does it appear they felt?
6. Review if there is something in your organization that a modified leadership approach could positively affect.
7. Analyze that and determine what can and should be done.
8. Determine an action plan that will improve the situation identified (what, where, when, how, to whom, etc.).

Principles For Smoother Operation

In the activity just completed, you attempted to address a situation and settle it in a better way. You did that without much ammunition, as it were. So now let us provide further information.

What to do? Remember, you are the leader. Remember that true leaders do not take energy from the group; they create it. No matter how cantankerous a person or group may be, remember that your objective is to be the catalyst in their growth and productivity. Of course, like most good advice, it is quick to write and easy to read. It sounds great until you have to solve a real problem or get into the middle of one of those really nasty confrontations. Let me help with some basic guidelines.

First, a caution: in viewing and attempting to make these principles part of your operation, do not make them a "five-day diet" program. That is, a quick try, followed by a return to the same old habits. As in successful dieting, you must think in terms of a lifetime commitment. Just as in dieting, continual hard swings from one idea to another and back tend to confuse the system and, in this case, the workers. In your organization, aborted efforts can provide less confidence and greater resistance to change. And I emphasize *can*. The other side of the leadership-trying-to-change coin, is that honest, sincere and open efforts, even if unsuccessful, can increase worker support and effort. The classic Hawthorn effect illustrates that in a profound way. If you are not familiar with it, I suggest you do a quick review. The impacting discovery was that even when management made things worse for the workers, because the changes were perceived as an effort to improve working conditions, output increased.

Success takes time. Not only are problems frequently not created in a day, they also are not solved in that short time frame. Just like the example of dieting, reducing problems and increasing trust, support, and dedication does not happen overnight.

Our objective must be to develop an atmosphere and a process for success where differences do not turn into problems. Instead, they become vehicles for dialogue and improvements. It must start with you and now. Today, you can start laying the foundation for dispute minimization, and practicing a logical and human way.

One of the secrets to success is *consistency*. As we touched on this a moment ago, the more consistent you are, the less problem you will have. In fact, your workers are currently operating in response to the consistency you are, and have been demonstrating. To reduce problems and increase productivity, you must repeatedly demonstrate that you really are interested in people first and the organization second. As a result, when differences arise, your people will be significantly more ready to have you help and more likely to listen to your counsel.

A key word is *demonstrate.* I have viewed organization after organization that profess a people-first philosophy. They plaquer it on the walls, proclaim it in their advertising, and preach it meeting after meeting, yet fail to adequately practice it. I have heard worker after worker complain about this incongruity. In fact, as I have stated before, this is the message I hear over and over and over, more than any other. They believe that the organization leadership talks about consideration for people yet demonstrates that people really are not their top priority. The word "believe" is important here. Remember, it is not what is happening, but what is perceived as happening, that makes the difference.

Sometimes we hear the saying that talk is cheap. I would counter by saying that talk is *not* cheap. On the contrary, it is very expensive. It costs in ideas lost, worker efforts, staff turnover, reputation, and problems.

As a recap, if you are serious about maximizing your organization's effectiveness, you must embrace three principles: demonstrate, consistency, and time. From there, we can go into some factors in reducing conflict and in developing processes that increase the positive movement toward an effective team.

Decisions That Stick

In dealing with group differences and decisions, the rule is that the more people who agree with the practice, solution or whatever, the higher the quality of success, and the longer it will be sustained. The closer any solution can come to consensus, the more likely it will succeed. Obviously, the reverse is also true. The more solutions are mandated from the top without buy-in from the staff, the less committed are those affected.

The caveat is that as a rule, coming to consensus takes more time for the total groups to agree. However, the time it takes to stay with the effort and the resulting fidelity results in an ultimate savings. Differences, like a partially cured infection, tend to continue to flare up or stay in dispute. People who disagree usually do not perform at the level of which they are capable. The stronger the disagreement the more pronounced this can become, sometimes even undercutting the organization. The time and effort of getting the consensus of the players pays off.

Traditions and inertia can work for or against us. On the negative side, sometimes it is very difficult to break an established pattern, even if it is obviously limiting. As we swing through our complex jungle, our tendency is to hold on to the tried and true vine. We know where it goes. We know it holds our weight. And it takes a certain faith and trust to move onto a different one. On the other side, if we can establish productive traditions and patterns, they too, can become a positive inertia. Establishing a tradition of openness, honesty, consideration, and working together will minimize differences and result in their having less impact. Also, fewer disagreements will escalate and move up the next step of intensity. Of course, regardless of your efforts, there will always be some disputes. That brings us to a way of dealing with those difference and disputes in the most productive way.

> **Humans are not pieces in a puzzle or cogs in a wheel, but feeling entities with unlimited potential.**

Dealing with Issues

In formal bargaining there are at least two basic styles—integrative or cooperative, and distributive. Although we are not going to focus on the details of bargaining, there are many components that are part of every interaction, and, if understood, can be used in all kinds of differences. The thesis of this book is that humans are not pieces in a puzzle or cogs in a wheel, but feeling entities with unlimited potential. And they also make decisions based on some sort of reasoning. We may not be aware of that reasoning. Even if we are, we may not understand or agree. However, remember, all individuals do what they do for a reason. On that platform, we build a better way to solve problems. Instead of ignoring that reality, to be maximally successful, we need to be aware and pay close attention to those reasons.

> **Everyone does what he or she does for a reason.**

Distributive Bargaining

Although we may not know it by that name, distributive bargaining is usually the image one thinks of when the idea of reconciling disputes or bargaining comes up. Distributive bargaining focus on issues and defines parameters early in the process. It is like dividing a pie. First, the size is determined, then it is basically a matter of how it is going to be divided.

For example, the department head says to the CEO, "I have to add three people to my staff if we are going to get everything done."

"THREE PEOPLE?!" the CEO returns. "You need three people?" I don't think I can possibly give you any! In distributive bargaining, the size of the "pie" has now been set. The range is somewhere between the minimum—none, and the maximum—three. While the department head may come back with a "Come to think of it, I really could use five," three will be the maximum he will get. This is such a common system that you experience it everyday. You go to a restaurant. You want Russian dressing on your salad. The waiter tells you they only have ranch and blue cheese. The parameters have been established. You either have one of the two dressings they have, or have none at all. That is the pie. In that situation, unless you get up and walk out, there are no other choices.

Using our first example, the CEO says that the display needs to be finished by next week. Knowing what it will take for quality, the department head replies that the only way she can get it out on that timeline with the people she has, is with serious quality compromises. Using the distributive bargaining practice, new parameters are set: quality verses time. Actually, our pie could be considered to be at least three dimensional: quality equals time and people. For example, if the time cannot be extended and maximum quality is most important, additional people will be required. On the other hand, if time is less critical, the quality could be achieved with fewer people working over a longer period.

There are at least two concerns in dealing with problems in this manner. First, it is not conducive to creative thinking; those involved tend to polarize quickly. Thus, for maximum creativity—thinking outside the box—this is not the best process. Second, there is a tendency to become negative and adversarial. Sometimes a zero-sum mentality develops. That is, in order for me to get something, you must give up something. Reasons, situations, feelings, and alterations are often not main actors in consideration. It is predominantly a *what*, not a *why*, system. Obviously, in solving problems, *what* has to be a consideration. However, under this system, interests are neglected, even though interests tend to be more personal and create feelings and contribute to better or poorer performance. Thus, this is very ineffective at improving support, building cohesiveness and maximizing human potential. And, in my observations, it is a poor vehicle for working with differences. In fact, it frequently creates them.

Change Activity 48

Although it has limitations, distributive decision making is not a bad or wrong system. It is only a limited system that, if not carefully used, can result in negative outcomes. As you do this next exercise, you will notice that somewhere in many decisions, distributive bargaining plays a part. For example, in the illustration used requesting more help, regardless of a different approach, eventually the CEO and the director must come to a decision on at least how many people and how much time are needed. However, how that point is reached is key to a cooperative attitude and increased productivity; we will delve into that next.

Sometimes we think of bargaining in a confining way—labor disputes, for example. However, distributive problem solving plays a part in so many of our interactions that it is important you readily recognize and understand how to work with it. To help that awareness, I am asking you to notice its prevalence in everyday life. Take a moment and identify at least one issue in the categories below that has been decided using the distributive system. If you cannot think of examples, you may need to go back and re-read some of this chapter.

Issue/situation	Identified distributive part
Home	
The Organization	
Other	

If you really had to strain to find some distributive bargaining, maybe a few more examples will help. First, the most obvious is at the car dealer's. The car you want is marked $20,000. You can't pay that amount. So you begin the dance by making that announcement. The sales person asks the next, "How much can you pay?" It goes from there. At this point, however, the outside barrier—size of the pie—has been determined; it cannot be more than $20,000. After the sales person's efforts at reducing the price, it would be amusing to watch his or her reaction if you said you would take it for $22,000. At home, the kids want to watch a TV show. One of their jobs is to do the dishes. You say they may watch after they do the dishes. The outside diameter of the pie is now set at "doing the dishes." They are not likely to extend it by asking if they may mop the floor, too. They may bring the side in, however, with a plea to do only half before the show and half after, since it starts in ten minutes.

Start looking and you will see that this system goes on everyday in situation after situation.

Change Activity 49

Find at least one more distributive bargaining situation that does not deal with money.

Cooperative Bargaining

Integrative or cooperative bargaining is a system that focuses on interests or why the party is making a stand at a certain point. In the example above, this would be why you will not buy the car for $20,000. It could be because you think $20,000 is too much for that car. It could be that you do not have the money to pay that price. It could be because you have decided that regardless of the car, you would never pay that kind of price. It could be any or many factors. The point is that everyone makes choices based on some reasons or issues or interests. Cooperative bargaining takes those as important considerations.

Although parameters may eventually be set, in integrative bargaining, examination of all possibilities is more likely to happen at the first. Using our original example, the department head says to the CEO, "I have to add three people to my staff if we are going to get everything done."

"Three people?" the CEO returns. "You need three people." He continues, "things are tight, but tell me more."

This is where the examination of *interests* and understanding begins. It is a time when the CEO's skills are required. He or she must for a time put aside his or her strong opinions and be open to listening to the ideas of someone else. This may be difficult, especially if the proposal of the other side seems absolutely ridiculous. It may require significant effort merely to go through the motions. However, going through the motions is a start. In addition to solving problems in a way that makes things and people work better, cooperative bargaining is also an opportunity for the improvement of communications, relationships, and the development of individuals and ideas.

Because you are looking at the situation from more sides, reviewing interests will produce truly synergistic ideas. The end result can be a stepping stone for totally new concepts, products, or what have you. That is in addition to the improved likelihood that you will come up with not just a solution, but the best solution. When everyone catches the vision and starts operating with real concern, this process becomes infectious. It has been my experience in using this approach that consistently, positive results and relationships develop well beyond my expectations.

Getting back to our example, by asking why and considering the opinions, ideas and problems of the department head, the CEO is also developing confidence within that person, essentially saying, "You are an intelligent and capable person; your opinions and views are valid."

This also places responsibility on the department head, essentially shortcutting the probability of blaming and backroom grousing. When the decision is made as an outgrowth of a collaborative effort by the CEO and department head, the department head bears a significant part of the responsibility.

I used to find union leaders' response to my concerns of costs for their proposals of, "That is your problem." That changed when I began sharing all of the situations and needs, and encouraged them to put all of their interests on the table too, and invited them to help make the final decisions. During a meeting, for example, it would be totally appropriate as part of the discussion for the CEO to share the problem this staffing request creates in the overall scheme of things, and to ask the department head for his/her recommendations for solutions. It may be that the individual's suggestion will impact some other part of the organization. If that is the case, you must point that out. If this is a serious consideration, a representative from the affected group should be involved. Two important results will emerge: (1) worker assumption of responsibility, and (2) disputes will stay fixed and fewer will appear.

Listening to and viewing many individuals—professionals to line people—and in many different organizations, I have noted how frequently and consistently they blame the leadership for whatever. In fact, they even blame leadership for things with which leadership has nothing to do. If you have been a leader very long, you have probably noticed this phenomenon with some consternation. It is because all of these people *perceive* that leadership has the power to fix things, yet does not. They frequently tie that to a reason and belief that leadership really does not care about everyone else or their ideas or their situations.

When I share that with leaders, their usual reaction is defensive, followed by a list showing how many things they have done for the workers, e.g., bonuses, gifts, employee of the month, extra benefits, etc. Frankly, my experience and a review of others show that these things do not make a lasting difference. Once again I restate that it is *perception* that determines our opinions. It is not what you do, but how they view what you do. Some of those perceptions can be 180 degrees from the truth. Even after working with both sides in many situations, I am still amazed at the difference between the intent and the perceived intent. Dealing from people's interests helps find out what really does make a difference. That, in turn, becomes the footings on which to build a better final structure.

Perception **determines opinions.**

I am convinced that there is one thing that would reduce problems, increase morale and productivity, and result in an improvement to the flow in any organization. It is for leadership to treat managers and workers more as competent, intelligent individuals, and openly encourage and consider their opinions and ideas. Although I see an honest effort in some organizations, in most it does not get to the point of effectiveness. Think of it as truly treating others as you would like to be treated. Do not translate that to "as you *expect* to be treated." There is a significant difference. And *truly* means genuinely and sincerely respecting their opinions, and actually giving them power. This concept is important in settling differences. The best solutions will come when everyone understands not only the facts, but the reasons, and accepts the feelings coming from each group or individual.

In meeting with your people, do not come up with solutions. Listen to their concerns without being defensive. Do not talk, listen. Be careful of high-emotional situations. Give people enough time to get it out and settle down. If you are verbally attacked or blamed, keep your cool. It may even be appropriate to have a cool down session, or a return meeting at a different day or time. You may think you have the perfect solution; hang back. Be a sounding board. Do some reflective listening; paraphrase back to them what you think they are saying. Listen for their central interests.

Find out the *whys*. I cannot over emphasize that it is critically important that you put aside your position and position thinking, and honestly consider their thinking and their interests. Listening does not mean you have conceded an issue. It does not mean you necessarily agree. So take that hat off for a moment, relax, and discover what they have to say. Try to identify their process interests, substantive interests, relationship interests, and interests in principles.

At this point I can almost hear readers thinking that this process takes too much time, isn't necessary, and sounds pretty "touchy-feely." Twenty years of leadership experience has proven to me that it takes less time and money than traditional negotiations, grievance hearings, dispute resolutions, strike management, legal depositions and lawsuits. Additionally, problems stay fixed. It is not only good personnel relations, it is good business.

> **It takes less time and money; it is good business.**

Do not assume that your view is their view. In my experience, a frequent contributor to less than optimal performance, worker dissatisfaction, and marginal settlements is that leaders assume they know what staff thinks, what workers want and what is creating problems. They sometimes make those assumptions based on little real evidence and without actually asking the staff. Unfortunately, they often make decisions based on misinformed beliefs.

Do not let your prejudices dictate your actions. You may know the chief negotiator, for example. Your previous interactions and experiences may jaundice your view. Perhaps, in your opinion, the only thing that would help him or her change opinions would be a long walk off a short pier. Many negative experiences may make it impossible for you to think or feel positive. However, as I have stated before, while what you think may not be helpful, it is your actions that make the final difference. Be careful. Once you say or act—play your cards—it is difficult to disavow the connection. You usually cannot put them back in your hand. If need be, write out every step of your way so that you present yourself and the process in a positive manner that will set the stage for a productive settlement. Remember that in all of those disagreements, the other half, your opponent, probably developed an opinion of you similar to yours of him/her.

Let me walk you through an interest-based process using a simple example, doing the dishes.

First, there is an *issue*—who is going to do the dishes. This is an issue that will not go away. After all, the result of not doing them will be that there will only be dirty dishes to use. There will be contingent problems, like the mess, the stink, and the overall home environment.

Second, there are *positions*. In this case, this is easily defined. No one wants to do the dishes. When translated, that means *you* do the dishes. That equates to the disagreement: I don't want to do them; I want you to do them. Which reciprocates as: you don't want to do them; you want me to do them. Unfortunately, at home, and more likely in the organization, the dialogue stops here—the *outward* dialogue. At work, for example, the answer may be decided by power. That is, "I don't care what you want, do the job or pick up your pink slip!" That ends the discussion. Except for the *inward* dialogue and the sharing by the worker what he or she thinks about this #%*# company and that #%*# boss. The result is that the player keeps playing the game but not at the optimal level. The only "pink slip" in the dishes situation can be a devastating separation.

Third, look at *interests*. Ask the question, "why?" Do not accept the first answer as the final answer, but explore deeper to get to the real interests. Actually, a true "why" may not be apparent even to the person making the argument. In our dishes scenario it may start like: "I go to work every day and shouldn't be expected to work when I get home," or "that is a woman's work; I feel silly doing them." Of course, the other side of this equation might go on with such things as: "Oh great! What a neat job." "Your hours are 8:00 to 5:00 and mine are 7:00 in the morning until 10:30 at night!" And, "you mean helping your wife is unmanly?"

Although this disagreement does not seem to be getting more pleasant or creating a better relationship, at least there is the beginning of a view of how the other side sees the situation. If you watched carefully enough, you have identified some interests. For example, for the wife, the dishes are not the real problem. One of her real interests is the reduction of her workload. For the husband, we see that part of his concern is his perception of the job as inappropriate for a male.

By the way, an interesting side note: Depending on your own beliefs that may be tied to your gender, *glare* may be setting in. That is, for example, because of your own personal views on males doing dishes, you may have felt a bit of emotion coming to the surface. That is exactly what happens in many disputes. It is natural but it is also debilitating. That is why in some formal negotiations an arbitrator is used; he or she cuts through all of the emotions and attempts to get people looking at realities. An arbitrator can also reflect what he or she is hearing as issues. In your relationships with people in whatever situation, wear your inward sunglasses to keep those glares at bay. Back to our example.

At the point where we left our couple, interests were surfacing. Hopefully, there would be more discussion, and more interests and feelings would emerge. However, let us just take one component. Dishes appear not to be the real issue. In fact, as we really listen to what was said, appreciation may be the bottom line. That is also an expressed concern by employees in the business world.

In an organization, the best way to proceed is to start by first writing interests on a large sheet of paper or a board. In developing negotiations, think of it as a brainstorming session; anything that seems important is put on the list. Since the list can be long, there comes a point after everyone has added what they felt was important, that the group must together prioritize the list. That way, the most critical interests are the ones that will be addressed first. Notice that *together* the group makes the decision. Next, attach issues. Continue on until all of the issues that the group can think of are attached.

Fourth, *invent* all possible options. In the dishes situation, we narrowed the problem down to reducing the workload, but discovered that this is only part of the problem, and that appreciation is probably a driving force. However, the feeling of appreciation is connected to a number of actions and must be considered throughout a spectrum of situations. It helps to acknowledge that feeling, but there must also be some actual change in the condition of reducing the wife's workload. If this were a labor dispute or a grievance, merely saying that you appreciated the problem or the need would not be enough. Thus, while underlying basis for actions need to be addressed, solutions must also result.

Back to reducing the workload—they might use paper plates, hire a maid, etc. In the organization, with a group or individual, this is another brainstorming activity. Thus, anything is allowed, even if it may not be practical. Again, this is an opportunity not only for participation by both sides, but also the development of a truer picture of a more complex set of drivers. This is sometimes an activity groups or individuals want to avoid. This childlike (we see it often in children) reaction basically says that I really do not want to know the complexities or what keeps you from taking care of the situation; just fix it.

Becoming practical is a process that requires both parties to look at their solutions to the differences. This works very well in a group. While two individuals can become entrenched in their own opinions regardless of practicality, when brought before a number of people together it is usually impossible to keep the absurd on the list.

Fifth, *determine* real options. It is time to discard options that are not practical at this time in this experience. In our dishes example, it may financially be totally impossible to hire a maid. That, then, must either come off the list or an alternate must be determined to allow that expense through reduction in financial obligations somewhere else or increased revenue. Financial constraints are a factor in many organization problems.

Sixth, *develop* a list of options that are most practical and that those involved could accept. Workload reduction, is an important interest in our example. Perhaps together they could develop a profile of the jobs that would reduce the workload on the wife, without violating the values of the husband. That is, if doing dishes is really an emotional issue with the husband, then maybe they can work something out that would not violate the value (right or wrong) while still meeting the needs of the wife.

Seventh, <u>together</u> *evaluate* from all of the acceptable options, the best possible solution. In our example, the evaluation might end up something like: "Gosh, I would be happy to vacuum and I can also give the kids a bath every night; I need to spend more time with them anyway."

In summary, our couple *together*—an important point—has separated the issue from the outward complaint (dishes from workload), discovered an underlying interest (appreciation), and developed solutions more palatable to both people. In the incident, they have also begun using a process that can be applied to other situations that will surely arise in their relationship. Of course, it would have been more simple to allow the contention to continue and still fight over the dishes.

Some organization leaders have told me they prefer the latter solution—settle the differences quick and in their way. They believe my recommended process takes too much time. They also believe it gives away some of their power. I can partially agree; it does take more time *initially*. However, as I have already noted, focusing on the most important bottom line, people, results in the improvement in the other bottom lines. Maximum production, profit, and reduction in disputes are just a few of the increase of time efficiency created. While taking time, it produces more for the time spent than any other system. The real evaluation of actions must be seen in a longer-range vision than the week's events. Additionally, developing a process that can be applied to many situations, and people who can operate the process, saves time in decision making.

The fear of giving away power is often more prevalent than supposed. Particularly in the business world, and in mid-sized companies, this is a common theme. It is usually not expressed in those words. However, the actions of leadership illustrate the belief. As I have indicated in earlier chapters, leadership that is afraid to lose power is not leadership that will optimize production nor maximize the potential of the operation. Again, position may be determined by decree, but the most effective leadership and the greatest power are not demanded; they are bestowed by followers. Additionally, processes using the intelligence of others encourages growth and ideas, which move the organization forward at a more rapid rate.

Our example of dishes is tame when contrasted to what happens in many organizations. It was used for ease of illustration. Because there is not as compelling a tie in organizational relationships, real interests often never surface. Often, both sides look at the other as negative, unappreciative, inept, and blind. Having worked with both sides—leaders and workers—at many different levels, I have seen how entrenched individuals and leaders can be. I also see how counterproductive and painful this is. Organizations spend millions of dollars trying to improve, yet fail to take some simple steps that would yield significantly better returns. Maximizing people requires focus on what *really* drives them, not on what we *think or traditionally believe* drives them.

At the end of meetings with groups or individuals in your organization, be sure that there is an accurate understanding of decisions and timelines, or what is expected in the next meeting. Have someone put it in writing. Since each of us brings to any meeting our own way of thinking, and since time tends to erode what has happened, this is important.

Follow up is important especially if something was said in a meeting that may have created negative emotions, or felt like a negative strike. An individual may have said something they felt that you felt was inappropriate. Often those items become larger in the mind than they really are. This is a golden opportunity for you to illustrate your true concern for that individual. Actually, it is a help to have some of these situations happen to provide you with these opportunities. Your visiting the individual or individuals in their space or mixing at events soon after your discussion will bring a relaxed assurance and will ensure a continuation of positive relationships. This is the leader's responsibility. You are the one who has the power. You are the one who makes things work. You are the one who sets the stage for the growth of individuals under your stewardship.

> **Leaders set the stage for the growth of individuals.**

A caution: when people share what really bothers them, how they really think, or their real interests, they need to feel safe. As discussed in a previous chapter, respect their thinking and their feelings—even if you disagree. A snide remark or a roll of the eyes negates all of your overtures to working together and respecting their ideas. I have worked with a number of individuals who just seemed compelled to make some statement or show some sign that illustrated their lack of respect for the expressed interests of those with whom they disagreed. In those situations where a team was involved, I have counseled these people not to be involved. If you do not treat others the way you would like to be treated, if you use them as jokes, you will have created something worse than you had before. In exploring interests or ideas in any situation, no idea is stupid.

Summary

All of this may sound condescending to you, or like playing a silly game. After all, these are not children you are dealing with (unless, of course, they are; these things work well with children). You may reason that these people need to accept the fact that life is not always kind. Very bluntly, I must say that that attitude is the very thing you need to change. I have seen that attitude result directly in the loss of millions of dollars, and indirectly, millions more. I have seen it cause considerable stress and enumerable problems, and the loss of positions and jobs.

This process does not weaken power. In my experience, the opposite is true. Power is much like security. Both of them are not found outside of us, but within. As previously noted, this way of thinking does not eliminate reality. Real life is still real life. However, when you work together to address those real problems that are part of your organization, whether it is money, relationships, product, market percent, or even the dishes, more people accept the determination, assume responsibility, and more willingly put forth greater efforts, resulting in the important bottom line: optimal success. Relationships are less likely to be damaged, and are almost always improved, and a true team effort is not merely feigned, but becomes real. And your profile as a leader is decidedly improved.

Application

We have just passed through a chapter that defines a complex and dynamic process. My recommendation is that you look for a simple dispute and try this process. Doing an exercise is like swimming, you have to actually get into the water before it can happen. If you are going to deal with significant issues, such as negotiations, I suggest you practice this process with your leadership team. Pick a problem that creates different opinions and take the process step by step. Although you can have fun doing it, it is important that you actually follow through and use the decisions seriously.

<u>A very important note:</u> this is a time-consuming process. If you are a linear, cut-to-the-chase, let's get things done person, this will be difficult for you. You will be saying in your mind, "What a waste of time! We could have solved this situation with a one-line memo!" *That is the <u>very problem</u> upon which we are focusing.*

This is the utilization of a process that does not just produce a simple solution that is mandated by the top and followed at a 75% level at the bottom. This process changes the atmosphere. It moves the workers from a *have to,* to an enthusiastic 95% *want to.* This is the very essence of this book. A quick example: Yesterday, a lady was in my office talking to our Director of Operations. I knew the woman so entered into the conversation. I asked if she were still working for a certain company. Her response, although tongue-in-cheek, is the kind of negative response I continually get from employees of that organization. She said as if apologizing, and with a shake of her head, "I'm sorry."

The sad situation is that although that organization believes they have forged ahead and successfully made important changes, the producing section of their organization is at about a 50% level of support. *That* affects quality. The leader thinks he is leading, but the followers are not following. That is not leadership. *That* affects production.

I have outlined the important elements below.

1. Set aside enough time to at least complete one phase of the project, an hour or two.

2. Determine the ending time so that everyone can relax and expect to be there for the entire exercise and will also not worry about a requirement to finish, which could detract from the quality of the experience and the outcome.

3. Do any preliminary introductions if members are not familiar with one another.

4. Set the ground rules, i.e., there is no rank in the room, anyone may say anything without regard for repercussions, how the process works, etc. A note here: if there has been turmoil, or if leadership has

created an untrusting atmosphere, there will be un-believers. Hopefully, you have been doing the activities throughout the book. If you have, there will be more trust at this point. If not, as a leader, it will be your responsibility to continually and consistently demonstrate that at least in this situation, everything is open and okay.

5. The information needs to be visually recorded. Of course, that can be done in several ways—a computer projection, a white or chalk board, or large paper. My preference is the use of large sheets of paper. That way, it cannot be erased, anyone can do the writing and crossing off, and it becomes a more physical involvement of everyone. It can also be handy to have a secretary or clerical person record the notes so that they can be easily reproduced, organized and distributed

6. After choosing someone to do the writing in front of the group on the board, paper, or whatever, declare the games open. Request that anyone and everyone bring forth the interests they see regarding the topic at hand. Crossovers are encouraged—an item that would be considered a management concern but suggested by labor, for example.

7. On the board, paper, or whatever, have the scribe write all interests as volunteered by anyone in the group. For example, higher wages and profit margin. (This is usually found in labor versus management disputes.) Some may be very similar. As in any brainstorming activity, put all items up. The sorting process will take care of duplicates or very similar ideas.

8. When everyone seems to have run out of items to note, and the group agrees that there are no more related to this focus at this time, you are ready to close this part of the activity and move on to the next step. At this point, although the list is considered complete, advise the group that with agreement of the group, additional interests can be added. It is counterproductive to continually add new interests, so be as thorough as you can before moving to the next step. The only reason I add the possibility of additions is because sometimes during the total process, an important interest that was not apparent becomes so, and you may wish, with the consensus of the group, to add it.

9. Prioritize the list. Often there will be more interests than can be dealt with in the number of sessions and the time frame determined. Thus, it is important to take the most pressing interests first. If you use large paper to go through the process, you will always have a record of all the items and can assure the group that if they so desire, in the future those areas you are unable to reach during the determined time can be the starting points for later work.

10. Starting with the top of the list, individuals who recommended items for consideration should be invited to lead the discussion on their specific point. Of course, others are encouraged to provide input.

11. Under or beside these interests, attach issues that are part of the picture. Interests are the *what*. Issues are the *why*. Be careful that these are not confused. For example, in wage disputes, it always sounds like money and benefits. However, it is more than that. On the workers' side, the money and benefits are relative. How does leadership spend? Is it for jets for the executives? Is it for new machinery? Is it

for something that the workers perceive as showing that they are not as important as these other things? The bottom line in worker production and maximum cooperation is tied to a feeling of appreciation and the illustration of that by preferential treatment caring about the people, first, the business next. And, in their eyes, they are the *people*.

12. Discuss the interests and the issues. Are there other ways of meeting the interests than the current practice? The question that should drive the process is "What is going on here?" This kind of thinking has produced alternate methods of meeting the real interests. It has also saved businesses from destruction.

13. Determine solutions that meet the predominant interests the best. In my experience, because they see the total picture more clearly, the process often tends to help individuals and groups accept determinations better, and blame less.

14. Commit to and share those decisions and directions. Also share the credit. This is a team you are building. The quarterback needs to be good (you), but he won't get to the line of scrimmage if all the linemen refuse to block. And, like football, anytime the rest of the team is doing their job with a maximum and successful effort, you look even better.

13

BECOMING

> There is a great difference between leading and managing. Managers use energy; leaders create it.

My major fear is that the things in this book will not be done, that leadership will continue as they have, that the organization will never realize significant improvement in the total operation, including revenue. Unfortunately, my experience lends support to that belief. So before we get into "being," let me share what I observe and have experienced in the hope that it will get you to at least consider and do some of the things I have suggested.

In my experiences and observations I see: (1) mediocre and almost-great institutions that could be so much better; (2) very many people who do not like their jobs, dislike their supervisors, and have little allegiance to their organization; (3) a common theme of illogical, unproductive and uncaring practices; (4) the wasted potential of human beings; and (5) the absence of determination by many leaders to openly learn and change. In our Tarzan jungle, we have the disposition to hang on to our present and seemingly most comfortable and safe vine. Accepting a new vine can be dangerous. After all, it could break or put us in a more complex area. But then again, it also could be that the one to which we are attached could break, or just as unfortunate, stop swinging.

I keep seeing self-destructive modes of operation that warrant, in the vocabulary of today's teens, "Duh!" As disrespectful as it may sound, some are so clear that literally a child would do differently! In fact, junior high students I personally interviewed, when asked to comment on several given situations that we have observed in the grown-up world, unanimously responded with more appropriate thinking. Why is that? That is the question that begs answering. We are better trained and have more experience. It is frustrating to see what could be, yet is not: an organization that has great potential, a dynamic philosophy and on the right track, just sits there with wheels nearly stopped, not accelerating down the track. Examples are everywhere: a large retail chain that has in place a process that, if used appropriately, would maximize employee satisfaction and achievement, yet does it wrong and never receives the benefit; schools that are inches away from unlocking a process that would dramatically decrease the number of children dropping out educationally, emotionally, and physically; a school district that came within moments of excellence, then let it drop away; a CEO who really wants to be helpful to his employees and the business, but does not take the necessary step; a CEO who sends leadership to a very expensive program, then operates ninety degrees off course. On and on goes the trail.

Indeed, the frustrating part of my experiences is not only the organizations that are miles away from perfection. It is not just the leader who does not appear to recognize what really makes a difference to human beings. It is not merely the school that is entrenched in mediocrity. These are all sad to see. However, the most frustrating are the numerous leaders and institutions that are mere inches away from the prize, but it might as well be a mile. These are people and organizations that could easily be there, but are not. Often, they are somewhat aware, but choose not to look any closer. Some leaders are happy with current operation. Some do not realize the great difference a little change would make. Others cannot visualize what that change looks like. And some are fearful or do not know how to bring it about. Too prominently are those who think that everything and everyone else should change, but fail to look in the mirror.

It is perplexing to see the many gyrations and significant expense that organizations incur in efforts to improve personnel functions—everything from elaborate recognition programs to walking on coals—when the secrets to people success are tools they already have. As trite as it may seem, the basic *keys* to success and the development, empowerment and use of people in a more productive and positive way are founded on introspection and everyday logical thinking. These principles work in the smallest organization and the largest conglomerate. They work in businesses, professional offices, manufacturing plants, schools, churches, even homes. They are only steps away. While some leaders will move ahead, unfortunately, others will just keep doing what they are doing, spending money on elaborate systems, or not doing anything. The regrettable truth is that some leaders would rather keep looking for silver bullets or get on the latest staff development band-wagon, than become learners with genuine movement to serve the organization. Yet were I a sales rep and offered those same leaders a five to ten percent net profit increase through my product, they would be very interested; that is what I am doing. I am telling you that if leaders operate differently, the net result will be an increase in net profit.

The secrets to success are tools you already have.

That brings us to the emphasis in this chapter: the focus on leaders becoming. Your challenge is not to just become aware or know. Your task is not to direct or do. Your quest really is not merely to change functions and encourage others. Your mountain to climb is to transform you. Your real challenge is for you to *become*. That may sound a bit too much like a Merlin the magician or Pollyanna phrase. However successful your organization and the correct bottom line—people—become, they will only reach their potential as you reach yours. The general who directs his troops forward never inspires the strength, commitment and determination like the one who says, "Follow me." Of course, the nice thing about exhibiting what you profess is like the difference between lying and telling the truth; when you live it you don't have to have such a good memory. Of course, that statement telling you to become, is easy to write but not so easy to do.

Throughout this book I have attempted to get you to do things, to actually function as if you are the person who could make the most significant difference in the people and the organization. If you have actually done these things, you will already be on the track to becoming someone a bit different and somewhat more helpful and powerful than you were. If you have not, I am sorry. Not only have I wasted your time, I have not benefitted your organization. Unfortunately, I will also more likely hear the usual complaints from your workers and see the same old operation in your organization. That is your choice.

If, however, you have decided that what I have said and encouraged you to do really could make a difference, and you have made an effort to explore them, there are other things that can also help you *be*.

Serving

Fourth Generation managers…work together with other employees as partners to help develop better and better methods to get better and better results.[38]

—Brian L. Joiner

Leadership can be a great catalyst or a significant stumbling block. CEO's, managers, superintendents, boards, supervisors, department heads, and others who have leadership roles, hold the keys. Many are hard-working, well-meaning individuals who want to contribute and promote the best for their organizations. The reason for singling them out is that they are point people. They are the leaders of the flocks. They are the people who have the power to make changes, initiate policies, and move and focus people and organizations toward their potential.

Leaders have a subtitle: "teacher." The music composer, Stephen Sondheim once stated that when he heard the word teacher he would get teary. In the religious world a title used for deity and leaders is teacher. Impacting teachers serve their pupils.

Let me restate, something said in an earlier chapter:

…our role as leaders is to develop people. Morally, it is the right thing to do…there is nothing as important as being the catalyst in the growth of our fellow human beings. I say catalyst because we cannot actually grow others. But we can set the stage, so to speak; we can assist. In another light, however, "catalyst" is not completely accurate, since the definition notes that the catalyst affects other things but is not affected itself. My promise to you is that human catalysts are changed in a positive way. Thus, while you are growing others, you are growing yourself.

Traditionally, we measure how valuable something is by its returns. In the stock market, for example, the stock that sells at the highest rate is considered, at least at the time, to be the most valuable. Unlike stocks and bonds, the most prized commodities do not change—they retain value as a constant.

Leadership is an everyday part of life. It makes little difference the setting—whether work, home, clubs, church, or what have you. In leadership as in any facet of life, measuring value is really quite simple: V=GR. The Value of something is equal to the Growth it Returns. When we give away things that are of low value, we have less ourselves. Low value does not mean low expense. When we give away things of high value, we actually have more. If we give money away, we have less. If we give friendship or love away, we have more.

It has been my experience that the higher values are not tangible; they are not commodities that can be put in the bank. They are also the most lasting; they don't suffer from depreciation. Often, these values expand and affect beyond our capacity to comprehend. When we develop people, we have started that unmeasurable chain. Not only have we impacted their lives, we never know how many lives they affect and how many others those lives affect—the chain goes into infinity. To be part of that process can be the most positive experience in life.

Although service may not sound like a worthwhile business move, remember: following on the tail of intangible rewards are those that *can* be put in the bank. That is, using correct principles will also result in increased productivity and business success. The final outcome wins on all fronts. Quality is quality throughout, not just on the surface.

My promise is that if you choose to employ this philosophy and actually put it to work in your organization, the end result will be greater achievement, less time and money spent on disputes, recruiting and retraining, increased efficiency, a more attractive financial bottom line, and generally easier operation. These are important benefits that result from building your people. The results will be a win for everyone.

To move in this productive direction, a critical element is the atmosphere you set. Let us take a moment and discuss a key component in gaining that atmosphere.

Inviting

If you want maximum success, you must (1) treat people as you would be treated and (2) think from inside their heads. The old statement that you can lead a horse to water but you can't make him drink, is important to remember. You can stick its nose in the water. You can drown the animal, but you cannot make it drink. You can coheres, you can demand, you can bribe, you can intimidate, you can force humans to do many things. You cannot force what they honestly think. You cannot force quality. You cannot force people to give the very best. You must set the stage and *invite*.

Dr. William W. Purkey talks about invitations and how they affect human beings.[39] He provides some guidelines. He classifies invitations four ways: intentional un-inviting, unintentional un-inviting, intentional inviting, and un-intentional inviting.

I view an *intentional un-inviting* leader as one who does not want input, has made up his or her mind, and has set forth a decree that had better be followed. If that is the way you operate, and if you decide that your middle managers will operate according to this book, you will expect them to know it and do it. If that is your approach, you missed the point. Re-read this book. Having worked under this kind of leadership, some of us listened, gave lip service to the process, and basically went ahead in the same manner we were going. In this setting, not only will the system not change dramatically, it will probably not change at all. Look around and you will see the carcasses of many ideas, philosophies and movements that had promise, but never got off the ground. If this is the kind of manager (sorry, but I do not call this *leadership)* you are, save your breath, it won't work. A bystander would notice nothing different, except, perhaps, more grumbling.

An *un-intentional un-inviter* is one who believes and talks about involvement, input, and the importance of everyone, yet his or her actions send a message that decisions and directions come from only one source. If you are one of these, you present the idea, allow discussion—although top the "good" ideas and suppress the "bad" ones—and end by implementing your ideas. Even though you may be sincerely trying to be inviting, you do not pull it off. Your actions may actually create more of a problem than your intentional un-inviter friend. Some of your people may begin to believe their input is valuable, but find that it really does not matter. For example, the superintendent of a school district determined a new approach for involving the community. It was discussed with the building principals. Then, a mandate was given that this process should happen by a specific date, and be done in a specific way. The idea was not a bad one. It had some very good aspects. However, because it was another mandate, a number of school implementations were very ineffective.

I have sympathy with this situation because, as noted above, some of these leaders are well-meaning. They want to initiate improvements. They have found something that has worked other places. They want to see that same success in their organization. If you are one of these, do what weight lifters and gymnasts do—have a spotter. Select someone who will be honest with you to evaluate your invitations.

There are also some readers who are probably thinking that not to operate by directing is not leadership at all. After all, leaders are decision makers. It is their obligation and right to determine direction and get the group moving. True…to a certain point. Remember one comment about leaders: if the people are not following, you are not leading. I might add: regardless of your title. A bystander would notice detailed instructions posted, people doing what was expected and with about the same feelings and excitement, or lack of, as usual. Or worse. The *or worse* happens because the program is forced. That often tends to create intentional and unintentional morale problems, lower enthusiasm, and less effectiveness. It often produces sabotage—intentional and unintentional. Remember how you feel when you are forced; others feel the same.

I once worked as a salesperson in menswear. I observed that the best way to sell was to set the stage and invite the customer to make some choices. For example, *telling* the customer that he *ought* to consider buying a tie with a shirt sometimes brought an added successful sale. However, moving the customer and his shirt next to the tie counter, holding up two ties against the new shirt and commenting that I couldn't decide which looked the best, more often resulted in him making a choice and adding it to his purchase. Not only did it result in more sales, it also increased the satisfaction of the customer; we tend to support and back our own choices better than those choices forced on us by others, even if the choice would have been the same. Promoting an idea and empowering people by allowing choices and latitude works best.

Un-intentional inviters in my thinking, are leaders who are positive, want people involved, but do not really plan for it. These are not negative, just not very effective, leaders. In implementing the philosophies of this book, these people share their thoughts and allow ideas from their people. But direction and execution tend not to happen. The default result is not negative, but it never reaches its potential. A bystander would notice an increased excitement and maybe some changes in some people and/or some processes. Or the operation might look much like it always had.

The *intentional inviters* are my favorites. These are leaders who are learners and who make significant efforts to skillfully present concepts, encourage discussion, ask for suggestions, and get consensus by the group on the best way and place to begin implementation. The *intentional inviters* empower their supervisors and line workers. That results in the ideas becoming part of these people, who are encouraged by the example of their leader to be intentionally inviting. These leaders may get volunteers who are willing to try first. In future meetings, they invite these individuals to share their experiences and make recommendations on alterations or improvements. In turn, the people who report buy in to the process more firmly as it becomes theirs. The more people invest their time, efforts and emotional support, the less likely the focus will fail. After all—as we sometimes say—no one wants to shoot down their own plane, particularly if they are in it. A bystander would notice an increase in enthusiasm, ideas being volunteered, changes happening, more people wanting to be involved and part of the firm or organization, and eventually an organization with greater success.

Sometimes, as with a number of recommendations that have been made in this book, leaders are not comfortable. They believe that the intentional invitation process takes longer; it seems inefficient. They visualize that it is an *everyone feeling good* flower-power approach. That inaccurate appraisal is unfortunate, will curtail progress, and cost potential success and money.

It does take longer to allow some to choose to move now, and some to consider maybe not even moving at all. In a way it would seem to be inefficient. Changing the atmosphere may appear that way. However, there is a point here that is not well thought through in so many organizations I have viewed. I have noted it throughout the book, but want to make sure it is plain here.

Be careful how you measure *efficiency*. It is kind of tied to *implementation*. For example, having all stores report that they have implemented the employee open-door policy by May first may sound like efficient implementation. And, if time and policy implementation are considered a success, they have met the mark. But what is the *goal* of implementation? Is it a time and a policy or is there another measurement that needs to be taken? What was the objective of the open-door policy? Is it having the desired effect? I use this specific example because in a certain group of stores, it is real. The idea is commendable. The efforts are well placed. However, for the most part, it makes little difference. I submit that this is not efficient and that the true intent and impact is not happening; actually, it has *not* been implemented.

In summary, true leaders do not stand with a whip. In fact, the very vision of that in my mind places the leader *behind*, not in front of the group. It is like the simile of sheep herding vs. shepherding used by Kimball Fisher in his book *Leading Self-directed Work Teams*.[40] Sheep herders drive subordinate flocks while shepherds develop and lead. If you really want to be a leader who makes things happen, consider carefully how you invite or un-invite people to follow you.

> If you are pushing your group, you are in the wrong spot for a leader.

The Bridge

…you'll have to give up being an administrator who loves to run others and become a manager who carries water for his people so they can get on with the job.[41]

—Robert Townsend Up The Organization

In the discussion in which we have been involved, the most effective leadership style takes the most skill, the most pointed focus, the greatest understanding of people, the best planning, the discipline to think ahead, and a demonstrated willingness to step aside and give others credit. The best leaders are able to motivate, even excite their followers. This should not be confused with charisma. Although it is nice to be charismatic, it is not the attribute that governs the greatest success. Indeed, Peter Senge, who has spent considerable time and effort examining leadership, notes in his *The Fifth Discipline* that the outstanding leaders of whom he is aware are not outstanding in looks, speaking ability, nor noticeable qualities. They are just very clear and persuasive in their ideas, continually open to learning, and have a deep commitment.[42] My experience provides a similar conclusion, only with an addition: the most successful leaders over the longest period of time are those who consider people first.

Of course, being the best and most successful leader is seemingly not the easy road. Actually, leadership, in and of itself, is not easy. It may seem at the time easier to be the commander who tells everyone what to do than the skillful leader who sets the stage, provides guidance, teaches, and empowers people. Remember that if you can get everyone on your big tandem bike peddling, your job becomes easier than if you just get everyone on your big tandem bike.

As a leader, you must become a bridge. You must be the medium to take people from the known to the unknown. You must be the escort to the edge of the light, to the edge of their security. You are the lead mountain climber; you have the opportunity to reach down and pull others up. Doing that takes considerable effort on your part. It takes faith in yourself. It requires you to venture out of your comfort zone. It necessitates you going up the hill ahead. You will find yourself, like the duck, trying to be calm and confident gliding along the surface while paddling like mad underneath. To most leaders this is not a new feeling; you have always worked hard and had to make tough decisions.

You have the opportunity to serve your people. The best leaders provide a service to those with whom they work. As we discussed in the leadership section of this book, the more you think in that mode, the more real you become, and the more readily people will follow. I repeat that this is your *opportunity*, your *privilege* to lead your people over the bridge. As an educator for many years, I had the rewarding experience of having a number of staff and students tell and write to me expressing their appreciation for the opportunities they felt I had provided—like a teacher who told me she had never had anyone place so much trust in her, and a long past student who related a positive experience that will remain with her forever. People-first leaders will receive those accolades, which are nice but not the point. They are merely verification that you have not only produced something, you have contributed to the development of a human being.

Acknowledgments are nice, but your greatest satisfaction will come by forcing yourself to stop and just observe what is happening because of your influence. Do not get hung up on the net profits or the gross sales. Take a minute and look at the development of people who have become more independent, more successful, more confident, more enthusiastic, and happier. If you have created the atmosphere and the structure, you see enthusiastic, learning and growing people. Once they have crossed that bridge, your task will be to stay out of the way and watch them accelerate.

Everything Was Always Possible

> Jonathan sighed. The price of being misunderstood, he thought. They call you devil or they call you god. What do you think, Fletch? Are we ahead of our time? A long silence. Well, this kind of flying has always been here to be learned by anybody who wanted to discover it; that's got nothing to do with time. We're ahead of the fashion, maybe. Ahead of the way that most gulls fly.[43]

> *Jonathan Livingston Seagull*—Richard Bach

Because it is so important, I choose to revisit this idea. Through all of the new inventions, ideas, philosophies, developments, there really is nothing new. That is, the same materials and possibilities, the same fundamental laws and dynamics have been here on this earth and in this galaxy since before you were born. They have not changed. The physics of flight, the laws of gravity and biological principles have been the same virtually forever. Those poor souls who traveled by boat down around the Cape for three months to go from one side of the country to the other, and those who chose the land route and struggled through the burning deserts and freezing snows to do the same, could all have taken either a modern air conditioned cruise liner or a jet and arrived safely and quickly at their destination; they could even have taken their oxen and wagons with them. Both were always possible. But as Stanley M. Herman put it in his book *A Force of Ones*,[44] "Only individuals can see beyond conventionally popular views, depart from consensus and stand for an unpopular position, generate a personal, driving vision that will inspire others to take a new direction, or risk resources and personal reputation to achieve a vision."

Limitations are in our minds, not the world around us. It is our understanding that changes. A different concept or a varied condition, a broken paradigm and a vision of possibilities are the things that have made a difference. As the great theoretical physicist, Stephen Hawking in his *A Brief History of Time* commented that scientific theory exists only in our minds and does not have any other reality. And any physical theory is always provisional, in the sense that it is only a hypothesis; you can never prove it. No matter how many times the results of experiments agree with some theory, you can never be sure that the next time the result will not contradict the theory.[45] So it is how we view things that results in opening the way for progress. It is a big step, and an important one. As Tom Peters wrote in his book, *The Pursuit of Wow,* "The first 99.9 percent of getting from here to there is the determination to do it and not to compromise, no matter what sort of roadblocks those around you (including peers) erect."[46]

But changing our view and mental determination are only part of the ingredients to success. There is another very critical challenge.

<u>Just Do it</u>

In discussions with many leaders, I hear agreement as to many of the things I have recommended. They can see the logic. They can see the advantage. They think that the concepts and changes espoused really could make a difference. Then Monday morning comes with its usual problems and tasks and these individuals find themselves operating as they always have. Or they may see the vision, but settle for something less.

Going back to our Applied Focus foundation, and as negative as this may sound, focusing is great—attending workshops, watching videos and reading books—yet, without application, without doing something, it is worthless. In the final analysis, what you read, what you see, what you feel, and what you think have little affect on others or the organization, unless you demonstrate it. So just *do* it.

Do not worry about the failures you could have or the naysayers who will say it is nonsense. In fact, those folks have always been there and railed against the greatest of minds and the most pregnant ideas. If they are telling you it can't be done, you may consider yourself in elite company trailing back to the beginning of time. Not trying is by far the worst failure. The naysayers' greatest claim to fame, since they cannot seem to come up with ideas themselves, is to hinder others.

Just take a few steps at a time. Actually, it is very logical and easy. The activities in this book were purposely set to make little steps so that you can experience a degree of success without leaving the safety of home base. Visit with some staff members who did not think you knew they existed. Ask some questions, listen to some answers, and really begin to hear what is being said. Then, take some actions that illustrate that you did hear what they had to say. Demonstrate that you are not merely a figurehead. Show them that you can be trusted. Be genuine. Be a leader.

As you do these things, you will find that they are easy, and that you will enjoy more what you do, and, like a bird soaring above, you will begin to see more than you ever have seen before. You will become a real leader; people will willingly and enthusiastically follow you. Your leadership will make a profound impact. *Becoming* is a significant word. *Becoming* is what life is all about.

Becoming is what life is all about.

Being

We have talked a lot about different things. I have suggested ways to operate. I have attempted to get you to look not only at what you do but how you view things. I have shared experiences, observations and examples. I now have one more concept I recommend you consider. That concept is *being*.

What we read and see are important. The kind of literature we spend our time with, the material we view on television, at the movies, and on the internet initiate or reinforce the way we think. The more we associate with these things, the more we become like them. We worry about the effects of these things on our children; they are as applicable to us.

In our association with others, we portray who we are by what we say and what we do. In our first dealings with others, we have only what we see and what they say on which to base our opinion. As we have discussed in the chapter on communication, our dress, countenance and gestures, coupled with what we say and how we say it, have affect. Although these cues as to who we are always have some influence, they are most impacting to those who know us least. For example, since I have a tendency to kid and make statements in jest, my wife has cautioned me many times that those who do not know me well, may misinterpret. That is wise counsel.

More important than what we say, however, is what we do. Actually, combined with what we say, actions demonstrate our inward fidelity. Unfortunately, we have experienced leadership that not only engages in inappropriate actions but adds to that offense by professing something different. As I stated much earlier in this book, it is better for these individuals to act true to what they have determined they are. At least people can count on their actions to match their talk. I would recommend, however, that if you fit in this bracket, consider making changes. As a leader, you are paid more, have more privileges, and viewed more critically. You can determine what you will do, but not the assigned consequences. You choose the benefits; you must accept the disadvantages. Much is expected of leaders. In my discussions with workers, the one theme I hear most often is criticism of leadership. Unfortunately, too much of it is deserved.

I cannot stress too strongly: walk your talk. While you stand to receive more scrutiny with the possibility of criticism, you will also gain a greater following and appreciation *if* you prove to be positively different. That story, too, is one told and retold. When, as they view themselves, the common people see motions by you that indicate you really do care about them, your stature climbs radically. So just do it, and do it now.

I started this section with the word "being." Being is the maturation of doing and becoming. Being is another one of those things like the measurement of value—the more you give away the more you have.

That is, it is similar to the light on your home smoke alarm: it is not noticed if you look directly at it. You have to look slightly away.

Being is something you become based on what you think and do. It is the lasting quality that people see as you. As people mention your name, they do not identify with what you read or watch. They may mention what you have done. But the feeling, the impression they have of you is what you *are*. That is what your being is to them and what being is all about.

Similar to the intangibility of *being*, is the method of acquisition. We may go out to *be something*, but our becoming who we are happens through a long process of many factors, influences, and actions. By utilizing the processes I have suggested, you will not only provide better leadership, you will *become* a better leader. And, like all good habits, it will positively change not just the lives of people with whom you work; it will also change your life.

Take the extra steps forward. Many times we learn about good ideas and we try to employ bits and pieces, but we just do not feel comfortable. It is not how we have historically operated. We do not want to consider changing our style. We fear that we may not be successful. People may possibly see our change as a ploy; they may not believe us. They will wonder what is wrong. They will have greater suspicion of our actions. As a result, many of us think good ideas, but continue to operate as we always have. Leadership has never been easy; it has always been uncomfortable and even unsure. "How do I work? I grope" Albert Einstein stated.

Studying and pondering are important to gain insight. Doing is critical if we are to make a difference. Being is the peace that comes when our thought and actions are congruent and become a way of life.

My promise is that if you develop people first—the right bottom line—the organization will rise along with them. There is no other focus, and no other way that will result in the greatest accomplishments or the lasting success and satisfaction. You have the ability. You have the opportunity. Your people need a way to get from where they are to where they can be. That is you; *do* things that make a difference and *become*.

NOTES

1. Peter Senge et al, *The Dance of Change* (New York: Doubleday), 1999.

2. Burt Nanus, *The Leader's Edge* (Chicago: Contemporary Books), 1989.

3. Val D. Hawks, "Looking Toward the Mark," *BYU Magazine*, (Winter 2005).

4. Sally Anderson, Ph.D, Organizational Development Consultant, 6492 N. Hillsboro Place, Boise, Idaho 83703, (208) 853-0073

5. Thomas A. Kayser, *Mining Group Gold* (New York: McGraww-Hill), 1996.

6. Douglas L. Ratelle, Ph.D, *Return to Excellence*, Seminar Workbook, 1997.

7. Thomas A. Kayser, Ibid.

8. Ray Stata, "Organizational Learning—The Key to Management Innovations," *MIT Sloan Management Review*, Vol. 30, No. 3, Spring 1989.

9. Peter Senge et al, *The Dance of Change* (New York: Doubleday), 1999.

10. Brian L. Joiner, *Fourth Generation Management* (New York: McGraw-Hill, Inc.), 1994.

11. Stehpen R. Covey, *The Seven Habits of Highly Effective People* (New York: Simon & Schuster Inc.) 1990.

12. Peter Senge, *The Fifth Discipline* (New York: Doubleday), 1990.

13. Burt Nanus, Ibid.

14. Robert Greenleaf, *Servant Leadership* (New York: Paulist Press), 1991.

15. John F. Kennedy, speech prepared for delivery in Dallas the day of his assassination, November 22, 1963

16. Peter Senge, *The Fifth Discipline*, Ibid.

17. Stehpen R. Covey, Ibid.

18. John Naisbitt, Patricia Aburdene, *Re-inventing the Corporation* (New York: Warner Books, Inc.), 1985.

19. Peter Senge et al, *The Dance of Change*

20. Foster Cline & Jim Fay, *Parenting Teens With Love & Logic* (Colorado Springs: Pinon Press), 1992.

21. Peter Block, *The Empowered Manager* (San Francisco: Jossey-Bass Publisher), 1987.

22. Thomas A. Kayser, *Mining Group Gold* (New York: McGraw Hill), 1995.

23. Tom Peters, *The Pursuit of Wow* (New York: Vintage Books), 1994.

24. Stephen Covey, Ibid.

25. Tom Peters, Ibid.

26. John Naisbitt, Ibid.

27. Robert Townsend, *Up the Organization* (New York: Fawcett World Library), 1971.

28. Robert Townsend, Ibid.

29. Brian L. Joiner, Ibid.

30. Saul D. Alinsky, *Rules for Radicals* (New York: Random House, Inc.), 1971.

31. Stephen Covey, *The 7 Habits of Highly Effective People*, Ibid.

32. Price Waterhouse vs. Hopkins, 490 U.S. 228 (1989)

33. Thomas A. Kayser, Ibid.

34. Robert Fritz, *The Path of Least Resistance* (San Francisco: Berrett-Koehler Publishers), 1999.

35. Brian Joiner, Ibid.

36. William W. Purkey, presentation to Idaho teachers, 1978.

37. Derek C. Bok, presentation, 1983.

38. Brian L. Joiner, Ibid.

39. William W. Purkey and John M. Novak, *Inviting School Success* (Belmont: Wadsworth Publishing Company), 1984

40. Kimball Fisher, *Leading Self-directed Work Teams* (New York: McGraw-Hill, Inc.), 1993.

41. Robert Townsend, Ibid.

42. Peter Senge, *The Fifth Discipline*, Ibid.

43. Richard Bach, *Jonathan Livingston Seagull*, (New York: The Macmillan Company), 1970.

44. Stanley M. Herman, A Force of Ones, (San Francisco: Jossey-Bass Publishers), 1994.

45. Stephen Hawking, *A Brief History of Time*, (New York: Bantam Book), 1990.

46. Tom Peters, *The Pursuit of Wow,* Ibid.

INDEX

A Force of Ones, 168, 175

Abstract, 56, 62

Accountability, 114

Albert Einstein, 171

All ideas, 133-134

Always leaders, 32, 40

Always learning, 13

Always possible, 12, 168

Analytical, 61-62

Applicability, 26

Application, 2, 4-5, 15, 18, 20, 24, 37, 40, 43, 45, 49, 54-55, 65, 69-70, 77, 82, 100, 104, 108-110, 120, 123, 126, 128, 130, 146, 158, 169

Application and Change, 5

Applied Focus, 40, 49, 121, 169

As a man thinketh, 56

Assume they can, 99

Assumption, 66, 99, 101, 121, 127, 152

Attention, 3, 13, 17-20, 29, 31, 40, 59-60, 75, 77-78, 82, 91, 100, 106, 112, 118-119, 121, 125, 133-135, 142, 149

Become, 1, 6, 8, 11, 16, 19, 25-26, 34, 39-43, 47, 58, 60, 77, 85, 88, 91, 97, 99, 105-106, 118-120, 139-140, 143, 145, 147-148, 150, 155, 157, 162-163, 167-171

Becoming, 24, 155, 161-163, 166, 170-171

Before you leap, 110-111

Being, 1-2, 9, 13, 17, 19, 25-27, 33-34, 39, 41, 45-46, 48, 58, 61, 64-65, 71-72, 75, 77-78, 83, 86, 88-89, 94-96, 98-101, 104-105, 108-110, 114, 117-118, 122, 125, 128, 131-133, 135-136, 139, 142, 145, 153, 161, 163, 166-171

Being human, 88-89

Bosses, 32, 95

Bottom line, xi, 1, 3, 5, 7, 9-10, 22, 40-41, 48, 54-55, 64, 71, 84, 98-99, 114, 117, 129, 131, 145, 155-156, 158, 160, 162, 164, 171

Brian L. Joiner, 12, 99, 163, 173-174

Bridge, 62, 167-168

Brief History of Time, 169, 175

Building on strengths, xi, 97

Burt Nanus, 3, 32, 173

Catalyst, 48, 91, 136, 147, 163

Chaining, 11-12

Change is difficult, xi, 121

Changes do not happen, 118

Choice, 8-9, 13, 23, 37, 55-56, 93, 102, 114, 133, 140, 163, 165

Coach, 47-48, 92-93

Common sense, 9, 22-23, 25-27, 29, 40, 45-46, 94, 96, 98, 143

Communicate all of the time, 104

Communication, 39, 78, 83, 86, 96, 101-112, 114, 116, 170

Consequence, 8, 142

Consistency, 65-66, 75, 77, 82, 85, 97, 120, 147-148

Convey importance, 2

Cooperative bargaining, 151

Cost of employee turnover, 51, 53

Counselor leaders, 41-42

Courage, 49

Dealing with issues, 149

Dealing with perception, 56

Decisions, xi, 17, 29-31, 44, 48-49, 57, 66, 92, 94-95, 99, 109, 111, 114, 122, 125, 131-132, 135, 139, 143-144, 148-150, 152-153, 156, 158, 160, 165, 167

Demonstrate, 118, 120, 147-148, 159, 169-170
Derek C. Bok, 139, 174
Developing people, 8, 41, 117
Differences and disputes, 139
Direct communications*****
Disney World, 117
Dissatisfied employees, 1
Distributive bargaining, 149-151
Do unto others, 94
Don't-bother-me, 145
Don't change, 6
Drill sergeant leaders, 41-42

Effective communications, 101
Efficiency, 108, 145, 156, 164, 166
Employees as partners, 163
Everyone equal, 132
Expandable assets, 71
Expectations, 6-7, 99-100, 152
Exponential quality, 48

Father-knows-best, 143-145
Fly on the wall, 16-17, 112
Focus, 1-6, 8, 14, 18, 25, 40, 42, 49, 54, 59, 61, 75, 85, 88, 102-104, 112, 121, 123, 126, 128-129, 131, 133, 136-137, 145, 149, 156, 159, 162-163, 166-167, 169, 171
Follow up, 39, 79, 114, 157
For a reason, 43-44, 149
Forced, 2, 98, 119, 131, 165
Foster Cline, xiii, 174
Fourteen Collaborative Principles*****
Fourth Generation Management, 12, 118, 173
Function, 41, 61, 96, 128, 163

Glare, 154
Global, 6, 61-62
GNSP=HLOS, 3
Goals, 42, 83, 120, 125-126, 129, 132
Good listening, 34

Growth, xi, 2-3, 5, 10, 40-41, 50, 83, 92, 104, 123, 126, 128, 131, 133, 140, 142-143, 145, 147, 156-157, 163-164
Guarantee, 5, 40

Habits, 15, 18, 32, 73-74, 76, 99, 101, 135, 147, 171, 173-174
Helicopter leaders, 41, 92
Higher = more impact, 80
Hinge principle, 2
Hiring, 19, 52-53, 97, 99, 144
Humanistic leaders, 143
Humility, 44-45, 49, 80

Ignorance influences, 25
I'm just a…syndrome, 4-5
Implementation, 31, 110, 166
In Search of Excellence, 99
Inconsequential concerns, 29
Indirect communications, 107
Infect, 2
Integrity, 45-46, 120, 133-135
Intelligent thinking, 23, 27
Intentional inviters, 166
Intentional un-inviting, 164
Interests, 90-91, 140, 150-157, 159-160
Inviting, 164-166, 174
Issues, 46-47, 61, 114, 140, 142, 149, 151, 154-155, 158-160

Jerk, 6, 39, 78, 96, 120, 132
John Naisbitt, 90, 173-174
Jonathan Livingston Seagull, 168, 174
Just do it, 15, 75, 169-170

Kimball Fisher, 166, 174

Leadership, xi, 1-2, 5, 11, 16-17, 19, 30, 32-35, 37, 40-42, 45-49, 53-55, 63, 65, 80-83, 85, 88, 90, 92, 94-99, 101-102, 104-106, 108, 111, 114, 117-120,

128, 131-137, 143-147, 152-153, 156, 158-159, 161-165, 167, 169-171, 173
Leadership reality, 55
Leading, 33, 80, 84, 95, 118, 134, 158, 161, 165-166, 174
Leading Self-directed Work Teams, 166, 174
Learner-teacher-learner, 11
Learning styles, 59, 70
Listening, 9, 11, 18-20, 30, 34, 48, 65, 70, 79, 84, 91, 96, 104, 112, 114, 136, 151-153
Logical thinking, 22-24, 27, 30, 40, 117, 162
Look at reality, 50
Love and Logic, xi, 41, 92

Making changes, 117-118, 145, 170
Managers, 3, 9, 20, 32, 35, 41, 49, 57, 92, 95, 99, 106-107, 118, 128, 130, 143, 145, 153, 161, 163-164
Managing, 161
Maximizing asset*****
McGreggor X-Y, 42
Meaningful changes*****
Meetings, 32, 79, 86, 88, 97, 111-112, 114, 121, 125, 133, 135-137, 139, 156, 166
Mining Group Gold, 6, 173-174
Misunderstood role, 33
Most difficult object to change, 121
Most important asset, 71, 94
Most important bottom line, 1, 7, 40-41, 64, 145, 156
Motivation, 91, 119

Names, 36, 41, 76-77, 89, 104, 132
New profile, 32

Observations, 1, 11, 17, 40, 72, 101-102, 150, 161, 170
Opportunity, 2, 40, 48, 61, 81, 109, 111, 119, 131, 137, 151, 155, 157, 167-168, 171
Options, 92, 155-156
Organization or insulation, 83
Own shoes*****

Patricia Aburdene, 173
Pay attention, 3, 13, 17, 19-20, 31, 40, 59-60, 75, 77, 91, 118
People are different, 58
Perceive through screens, 13
Perception determines, 152
Perception is fact, 56
Perfect, 11, 76, 88-89, 125, 153
Performance, 14, 99, 105, 124, 150, 153
Perspectives, 6
Peter Block, 49, 174
Peter Drucker, 47
Peter Senge, 11, 22, 32, 99, 167, 173-174
Planning, 47, 108, 121, 125, 132-133, 135, 167
Ponder and reflect, 140
Positions, 3, 33, 37, 53, 83-84, 107, 144, 154, 157
Power of perception, 69
Power of your position, 53-54
Price Waterhouse v. Hopkins*****
Pride, 23, 130
Privilege, xiii, 40, 168
Production, xi, 3, 5-6, 10, 17, 46, 48, 52-53, 61, 94, 114, 156, 158, 160
Productively, 143, 145

Qualities of leadership, 40-41
Quest, 10, 16, 126, 128, 162

Ray Stata, 11, 173
Recognition, xi, 2, 11, 33, 49, 66, 72, 77, 162
Reflection, 34, 74, 106
Re-inventing the Corporation, 35, 173
Richard Bach, 168, 174
Right bottom line, 5, 40, 48, 55, 171
Right questions, 134
Robert Fritz, 117, 174
Robert Greenleaf, 32, 99, 173
Robert Townsend, 91, 98, 167, 174
Rules for Radicals, 101, 174
Rules of the road, 130

Sacred dishes, 133, 135

Sally Anderson, xiii, 5, 173

Saul D. Alinsky, 101, 174

Secret to success*****

See what we expect, 13, 118

Self-fulfilling prophecy, 5

Sequential, 61-62

Servant Leadership, 32, 99, 173

Shared decision making, 17

Shrink people, 92

Significance of perception, 56

Smoother operation, 147

Sociogram, 35, 37, 132

Stanley M. Herman, 168, 175

Stephen Covey, 18, 32, 72, 88, 99, 174

Stephen Hawking, 169, 175

Styles, 33-34, 42, 48, 59-62, 70, 84, 143, 145, 149

Success, 1-3, 5-6, 9-11, 13, 26-27, 30, 33, 41, 45-47, 49, 53, 62, 71-72, 75, 84, 88, 91-92, 94-99, 105, 107, 119, 122, 124-126, 129, 131-132, 134, 143-144, 147-148, 158, 162, 164-167, 169, 171, 174

Successful leader, 167

Synergy, 7, 12, 126

Teacher, 2-4, 11-12, 22, 54, 57, 76, 95, 97-98, 142, 163, 168

The Dance of Change, 2, 173

The Fifth Discipline, 11, 32, 99, 167, 173-174

The Leader's Edge, 173

The Path of Least Resistance, 117, 174

The Pursuit of Wow, 169, 174-175

The sacred concept, 95

The Seven Habits of Highly Effective People, 18, 173

They are not following, 33

Think ahead, 23, 167

Thinking styles, 60-62, 84

Thomas Kayser, 6

Three perceptions, 63

Time, xi, xiii, 2-4, 6-9, 11, 15, 17-23, 25-28, 30-31, 33-35, 41-44, 46-48, 52-58, 65-66, 68-70, 75-76, 78-80, 82-86, 88, 91-92, 95, 97, 100, 102, 104-106, 108-109, 111-112, 114, 116-117, 119-121, 123, 125, 128, 132-137, 139-140, 143, 145, 147-151, 153, 155-159, 163-164, 166-170, 175

Tools, xi, 4, 6, 9, 37, 162

Tom Peters, 71, 75, 83, 99, 169, 174-175

Training, 2, 4, 19, 23, 33, 35, 46, 48, 52-53, 81, 91, 94, 109, 119

Trust, xi, 10, 31, 39, 43, 46-47, 49, 54, 65, 77, 82, 84-85, 95-97, 106, 112, 119-120, 122, 135, 147-148, 159, 168

Understanding your role, 32

Un-intentional inviters, 166

Un-intentional un-inviter, 165

V=GR, 164

Val D. Hawks, 5, 173

Validation, 84

Vision, 34-35, 41, 47-49, 90, 92, 118, 126, 130, 140, 152, 156, 166, 168-169

Water closet, 108

What you say, 96, 99, 105-106, 110, 134

What you think, 16, 76, 110-111, 153-154, 169, 171

Who we are, 76, 93, 121, 170-171

William Purkey, 131

Xerox, 6

978-0-595-41567-0
0-595-41567-9

www.ingramcontent.com/pod-product-compliance
Lightning Source LLC
Chambersburg PA
CBHW081146180526
45170CB00006B/1945